THE HOPE TRUCKLINE

AND 75 MILES OF WOMEN

BY
DENNIE D. McCART

Hope and Sunrise Historical Society
Publisher
Box 88 • Hope, Alaska 99605

T5-BCF-151

The Hope and Sunrise Historical Society
wishes to thank the
Dennie McCart family
for permission to
reprint this book.

The Hope Truckline and 75 Miles of Women
Copyright © 1983 by Dennie D. McCart
All rights reserved. No part of this book may be reproduced in any form or
by any electronic or mechanical means including information storage and
retrieval systems without permission in writing from the publisher, except
by a reviewer who may quote brief passages for a review.
Library of Congress Catalog Card No. 83-72535
Printed in the United States of America
ISBN: 0-9657315-2-9
First Edition 1983
Second Printing 2005

PREFACE

The Hope Truckline is a serialized chronicle of one man's adventures in a land apart—the great Alaska frontier. The vignettes contained within these pages cover approximately a ten year span of major growth and industrialization in the Alaska Territory.

Allow yourself to be transported back to the beginnings of a vital regional commercial network as you participate in the birthing of the Hope Truckline. Travel through years of hair-raising escapades, on the road and in the wilds. Spark to the gold rush tales of the Old Timers, and experience the historic placer mining efforts of the early 1930's.

As you walk through the pages of these simple tales you will become one with the extended family that has become the hallmark of Alaskan hospitality. Warm to the love, humor and good times of an era frozen forever in the hearts and minds of the men and women who lived it.

Read! Enjoy!

MAP

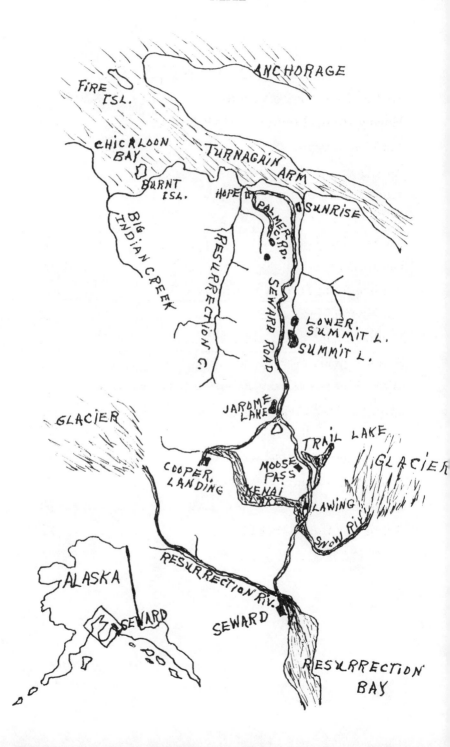

TABLE OF CONTENTS

THE HOPE TRUCKLINE

AND 75 MILES OF WOMEN

1

My Last Gold Mining Venture

It was a nice day in Anchorage, Alaska on May 12, 1938 when Bob Mathison came in with his 34-foot round bottom boat called *The Fiber*. It had a 4-cylinder Chevrolet engine in it, and about 7 knots was its full speed. He picked up a 40-foot barge from Emards Cannery and we took off at high tide down Cook Inlet to Fire Island. We threw out the anchor and waited until the tide had run out of Turnagain Arm.

We were at the tip of Fire Island waiting for the tide to turn. After the tide had been running back in for about two hours we took off up Turnagain Arm. It runs very fast each way from Fire Island and can take you back up Cook Inlet if you aren't careful and don't know the waters. Bob caught the tide all right. Boy! we were moving right along like going with a fast river current.

In about three hours we were getting into Chicaloon Bay and were on the lookout for the mouth of Big Indian Creek, which is hard to find when you are a mile out on the mud flats and have to go up the creek as the tide comes in. After about one hour of looking with binoculars and going back and forth along the mud flats getting the right mountain lined up with Fire Island we finally spotted the cut bank of Big Indian Creek. We could see the mining equipment that we were to pick up. I started sounding the bottom with a long pike pole. When I could not feel the mud under us we knew it was the creek channel and we headed right up the creek.

Bob put that boat and barge up that creek channel and along the mud bank where we were to load, just like parking a truck. He was right on top of the tide. We had no more than got big stakes and anchor out with the barge and boat secured, till the tide was running out of Big Indian Creek 15 or 20 miles an hour. It was not over 30 minutes until the barge and boat had gone aground.

We got busy rolling hydraulic pipe, up to two feet in diameter and 30 feet long, onto the barge. We had about three thousand feet of all different sizes to load; the Model T Ford truck; a derrick base, mast and boom 40 feet long; also 80 pieces of 30 pound railroad iron, three feet long, which was used for riffles in a sluice box.

It was dark when the barge was loaded and two very tired men had to get something to eat and grab a short nap. When the tide came in we were up and ready to get out of there as quickly as the tide was full. We wanted to be out from Big Indian Creek and up close to Burnt Island when we went aground. Now we could eat and have a good sleep for about seven hours.

When the tide put us afloat Bob headed his boat and barge toward Fire Island, which I thought was very odd. But it did not take long to see why. The tide was running so fast that we had a hard time getting out into Turnagain Arm before we would get shoved up on Burnt Island. When we got out from shore about one half mile the tide was taking us backwards up Turnagain Arm. Bob stopped the boat, pulled in the tow line, and then turned his boat around and started up Turnagain Arm with the tide, letting the tow line out on the barge slow as he took up slack. By now we were going up Turnagain Arm with the tide and power of the boat at a good speed. It seemed no time at all until we could see Hope, Alaska showing up. Bob was heading *The Fiber* into Resurrection Creek Bay. We got into the mouth of Resurrection Creek just at high tide by Bob Mathison's very skilled navigating and timing. When we got tied up, "Hurray, we made it!", and breathed a big sigh of relief. Now for some rest. This time I could work a little slower unloading the barge. There would be a couple of tides before Bob would take the barge back to Anchorage.

Turnagain Arm has next to the highest tide in the world, and when the big tides are running we have a 34-foot

Model T Truck and Hydraulic Pipe.

change from low tide to high tide. So about every six and one-half hours the tide is rushing up Turnagain Arm for about forty miles, or rushing out. It is a very fast and dangerous piece of water.

When the tide is going out, the tide coming in meets and creates a tidal bore. The water will pile up and roll sometimes eight feet high and three miles wide.

In the winter time I have seen the bore come in with big ice cakes five feet thick and twenty feet wide. They just roll over and over in the bore coming one hundred feet back, then rushing with the fast tide to just roll over and over again. You can hear the roar of this tidal action three miles away.

2

Moving Mining Equipment Up Palmer Creek

My job was to move all this mining equipment with this Model T Ford truck, four miles up a steep one-way mountain road (with a few turnouts) to Palmer Creek point. Then down the ridge for one mile where I then was to slide all this equipment down a steep three-hundred-foot bank, where we would set up for placer mining.

While moving the equipment up Palmer Creek I was to stay in a little ten-foot-square room with a bunk bed and stove, on the end of Bob Mathison's shop, which was across from the Hope General Store. There had been eight or ten kids down on the flats to see what was going on and George Roll, the man who owned the store, had also looked things over. I found out all the men were up the creeks and in the hills mining, except Joe Richards and Tom Tessier, who were sawing railroad ties about two miles out of town by Mud Lake. The women were busy growing gardens and taking care of the children.

The first week I would get up early, cook my hot cakes and bacon and eggs, make my lunch and drive up to Palmer Creek point; park the truck, then grub brush and dig out alders and birch trees making a road down the ridge for one mile. There was a steep hillside which I had to dig out. I spent weeks of hard work making a road where I would slide the equipment down to Palmer Creek. Ed Haun, my partner, and I had four claims staked out. Two claims were right in the canyon, just enough room to mine. The canyon there was one hundred to two hundred feet wide.

Ed, his wife and son, Ralph, were in Anchorage. He was doing carpentry work to be able to get enough money to keep me going and have a grub-stake. They were to come over to Hope when I notified them that the equipment was

5

moved. Then Ed would help get the hydraulic pipe put together and set up for mining and see if we could get some mining done before winter.

I had just finished the mile of road on the ridge and toook the Model T down for a trial run. The road was OK except where I had hillside-graded with a No. 2 shovel. I did not make it wide enough and almost slid off, so I had to do some more shoveling. I got back on top and was just feeling as big as Paul Bunyon ever felt for my accomplishment, when around the corner came another 1924 Model T pickup. He came to a stop and shouted over the howling wind and the Model T noice, "I am Iver Nearhouse. I have a quartz mine about three miles on up the road. Everybody calls me Doc, a handle hung on me when I was the first drugist in Anchorage when the town first started. My establishment was a tent."

After a few minutes of conversation he said "So long" and let the old Model T take off down Palmer Creek hill. It was an amusing sight. A two hundred pound man sitting in that little Ford, with it listing over a lot on the heavy side, the cloth top all loose from years of weather, flopping in the wind.

When I got down to Hope that evening I made preparations to start loading up early. Then I was to start the big job of moving all the mining equipment up to the designated spot on the hill where I would let it slide down a steep shale slope, three hundred feet, to the creek where we were to start our placer mining.

The kids around town dropped in to see me that evening. You could always figure on eight or ten of them for about a half hour visit. I was feeling pretty good about my progress so I asked if they would like to hear some music. They all said that would be nice. I took out the harmonica and started playing old time songs and a few hoedowns. They were a very good audience and really enjoyed my music (plus a few capers). I think right then and there I was an all right guy as far as they were concerned.

The next morning at 5 AM I was down on the flats loading up when George Roll came down to see what I was doing. In a short time I was on my way up Palmer Creek road, grinding along in low gear with a heavy load for a Model T Ford. She was doing fine, some steam coming from the radiator, but that did not foul up my vision as I had taken out the windshield. When in need of more water it was no problem as there were dozens of little streams coming down the bank along the road with nice icy cold sweet clear water to add to the radiator every once in awhile. I generally always took a sip of the cool water at the same time. You just stooped, or laid down by the stream, and drank. My nose, mouth and chin would feel kind of numb from the cold water. About two miles up the road there was a big meadow of grass and brush which was caused from snow slides wiping off the trees. It was June, and back next to the mountain there was still some snow. As the snow melted it kept the grass watered.

That morning I found out why they called it Moose Meadows. About fifty feet from the road stood a big cow moose and a calf. She only looked at me steaming up the hill. In just a few seconds she and the calf took off in a run into the brush. From that time on I looked for them every time I went by. Sometimes in early morning or late evening they could be seen.

I was very lucky on the weather, as anytime we had a light rain I could not get back up the road I had built on the ridge. But by the fourth of July I had about everything moved. The kids had informed me that all the men at the mines came to town and everybody (about 65 people, and a few dogs too) came to the Hope Social Hall, which had been built by all the miners and Old Timers in the early nineteen hundreds from big hand-hewn logs.

July 4th about 7 AM I noticed a few men coming in and out of the store. Business was getting pretty good over there. About 10 AM the kids had dropped in and said there was to be a dance starting about three o'clock in the afternoon. The women would bring food and everybody was to come.

When they said food I just got busy stropping up my straight razor for a good shave and getting my best clothes on for the occasion.

I was walking down the street about noon when a little fellow said "Hello! My name is Swede. I am headed down to the corner where Mitchells live. Come on down and have a cup of coffee and a sandwich."

Well, I fell right in with him. We went into this little cabin. Boy! it was just buzzing with lots of people and some kids. I didn't know anybody but it made no difference. The first thing I knew Mrs. Mitchell handed me a sandwich and some coffee, which I took willingly. I just started talking to everybody whether I knew their names or not.

After a couple hours of visiting everybody started leaving and going down the street to the Social Hall. All the ladies and girls were in their Sunday best dresses, bringing in lots of dishes and pots of food which were placed on the table over in the corner of the hall, by a big 110 gallon barrel stove. But the stove was not fired up at that time of the year.

On a platform about two feet high at the back of the hall were some men with bass violin, guitar, banjo and violin. I learned later they were the Clark boys; Delmar, Sobel and Hub (the oldest Clark, whom the boys called "Pap").

When they started playing it was just the kind of music that would almost make a dead man jump up and start dancing. Everybody danced, kids and all. Boy! what a wonderful time. We stopped to eat for about an hour and did I ever store away the food. Then back to dancing until about 9 PM. Then the men left to go back to the mines and jobs they were working on. I was ready for bed myself, and was so pleased to be part of such a nice community. Best of all I had danced and got acquainted with some very nice, attractive girls.

The next morning, July 5th, I didn't get up so early. I only made three trips up the Palmer Creek road that day. By July 7th I had all the hauling done.

I moved up on Palmer Creek where we would be mining. There was a little cabin about thirty feet from the creek which was built in 1916 by a miner. He had done some mining in a cut, shoveling by hand, and did not find the ground rich enough so he gave it up. The porcupines had been living in the cabin and chewing on everything that was salty or greasy. I had a job cleaning the place up, and patching the door to keep out the porcupines. The first week after I moved in I had the job of getting up at night and killing two or three porcupines which were determined to chew their way back into the cabin. I didn't feel like sharing my home for two months with them.

You can't imagine what I got into when I made a small, turned-up sled affair to fit over the ends of the hydraulic pipe. With a ten-foot rope tied to the sled I started to let a piece of this pipe down the steep 300-foot shale slope to the creek. Boy! Oh, Boy! the pipe took off down that slope like a scared rabbit, with me holding it back as best I could. I grabbed brush and little birch trees as I went sliding by, trying to hold down the speed. Sometimes I was stretched out like I was trying to fly, with the brush being pulled down and trees being bent over, then grabbing again.

It was no time at all until I was down by the creek with my first piece of pipe. Whooee! Safe and sound with no damage to the pipe. My arms felt like they were a foot longer, but after resting and thinking things over a bit I climbed back up for another trip. I only made three or four trips a day for a couple of days, until I got into shape and was not so stiff and sore in the mornings. After that I made all the trips I could stand in a long day. The days were long this time of year, you didn't have to worry about enough daylight to work in.

By the last week in July I wrote a letter to Ed, my partner, his wife, Ione, and son, Ralph, to bring some grub and come over. We were ready to set up the plant and start mining. They came over with Bob Mathison on *The Fiber*. I had a little one-room cabin picked out in Hope for his wife and boy to live in. It did not cost any rent as it belonged to no one in particular, just abandoned by some Old Timer.

Ed and I put up a tent right where we would start mining, and got busy laying pipe. We were making good progress when one day as I was digging a place for the pipe on a hillside, I got stung by a big black bumble bee, just above my left eye. Well Boy! I started out through the brush on a run, Ed right after me, and in no time my eye was swollen shut. We went down to the tent and started soaking my bee sting with soda. After about an hour of that we used vinegar. That took the fever out and I felt better. The next morning I could see out of my eye so we went up to where the bees had a nest in the ground. We made a torch with a old burlap sack with some oil on it, and burned the bees out of there.

Around August 12th we were ready to start mining. We had about forty pounds of pressure on the water with a big volume. Our monitors, or giants, were big tapered pipes about ten feet long with straight fins inside, called riflings, to keep the water from coming out of a four inch nozzle in a whirl. A solid stream is what we wanted to wash and push the gravel, dirt and rocks through the sluice box. You probably have seen fire fighters with a one and one-half inch nozzle blow shingles right off a house. Well, just imagine what a four inch nozzle can do. You can knock the bark off a cottonwood tree fifty feet away.

Ed piped the dirt into the sluice box, and I piped the tailings away at the end of the sluice box. Every half hour we would stop and lift fifty to one-hundred-pound boulders out with the hoist. Yes! that's why gold is so valuable. There is a lot of rock and dirt to move to get down to bedrock where the gold is.

We had just about got a big pit worked out fifty feet wide and one hundred feet long. It was about eight feet to bedrock. Ed had done some test panning in some of the most favorable spots on bedrock. He would show me a pan with some nice pieces of gold in it, as big as your little fingernail, and some fine gold too. He was one of those men that had gold fever; the more he looked at it, the bigger the gold looked. He would say, "Kid we are sure going to have a

Hydraulic Mining on Palmer Creek.

good cleanup", which made me feel pretty good after all this hard work.

We had only about an eight foot bank along the creek where we were mining, and on September 12th it started to rain real hard. It was raining harder up in the mountains at the head of the creek. About eight o'clock that night the creek started getting high and roaring like mad. We got busy and piled lots of big boulders along the creek bank by the pit. We were cold and wet when we went to bed. Sometime during the night I woke up; the creek was a lot quieter so I figured the water had gone down. But when we got up about six in the morning and looked out, Oh Boy! there was the creek running down through our pit within ten feet of the tent. The sluice boxes were just about covered with rocks and the giant at the end of the sluice box was covered with four feet of gravel. After two days of waiting, the creek got back into its original channel. We decided we had better clean up the sluice boxes as soon as we got them dug out and could get the riffles up. We had learned from a man from Brenner's mine that the water had done lots of damage at their diggings; and the Clark brothers, who were placer mining on a lot bigger scale, had some high water problems, too.

3

The Gold Cleanup

This was the big day. Ed and I started cleaning around the head of the sluice box, spotting a little nugget every once in awhile. Then we started to lift up the riffles, and there was a pretty good looking streak of gold showing up across the box. Ed was really excited; in fact, I was starting to feel like all this hard work was getting its rewards. After about two feet of riffles had been taken out and very little gold was showing up, my heart began to sink and Ed was not talking so fast. By the time we got twelve feet of riffles out our hopes had been shattered, anyway mine were. Ed still had that old prospector's feeling, "Kid, it's here, we will get it in the next pit".

We had a little over four hundred dollars worth of gold for all that work. Gold was only $26.35 per ounce at that time. Winter was getting close and there was no use in trying to mine anymore that season. The creeks would be icing up within two weeks.

There was a contractor from Juneau starting to build a schoolhouse in Hope who needed another carpenter, so Ed went to work for him.

I was lucky enough to get a job with Earl Clark for two weeks. Earl was in a hurry to have one more cleanup before winter stopped the mining. Earl had a big hydraulic setup, with ten men working for five dollars a day plus board and room. We worked ten hours for a day's pay at that time. I was very pleased to get this job as it would give me a grubstake for the winter. It was a sight to see when Earl had his cleanup. Whoo-ee! right around three thousand two hundred dollars in gold. By then there was ice on the rocks and everything started to freeze so everybody went to Hope to hole up for the winter.

13

4
First Winter in Hope

I was lucky enough to rent the Plowman log cabin for ten dollars a month. This was a nice big cabin and somehow became the main get-together for all the young men. We gathered to tell tall tales of our experiences hunting, and of course, women, which seemed to be a very important subject, too.

One afternoon there were about six guys sitting around gabbing. I think they hung out at my place so as to get out of work at home; also I kept plenty of wood around and the cabin warm. This particular day Eddie Brenner had to go out to my outhouse, which was pretty nicely made from split shakes. Right away someone suggested we upset the toilet while Eddie was in it. It did not take us long to jump up and sneak out around the back side of the outhouse and tip it over with the door down. There was a lot of hollering and laughing going on and when Eddie stuck his head through the hole of the seat in the toilet pleading for us to let him out, it was a sight that would make your mother-in-law laugh. I don't know why I was laughing so much. Gosh! it was my own outhouse that was upset. After about thirty minutes of fun we all lifted the outhouse back up and let Eddie out but he had to promise to forgive us. I don't think the outhouse was as solid or level as before but I was happy to have it set up and ready for use when nature called.

One evening I shaved lots of flakes of naptha soap into a tub of water and put in my clothes to soak until morning. Every once in awhile I would tromp them with a hobo, or sourdough washing machine. It was a one-pound coffee can with a few holes on the sides and a two-foot broomstick for a handle. You worked it up and down on the clothes, and with its suction action in the water it did a good enough job of washing clothes without rubbing the hide off your knuckles. The next morning about ten o'clock I took the washtub outside by the cabin. It was a nice, warm sunny day. The air was so clear that all the mountains looked higher and closer than usual. All at once I noticed a white spot up among the rock pinnacles on Porcupine Mountain. This mountain is about three thousand feet high just to the north of Hope. After a couple more splashes with the sour-dough washing machine I dropped everything right then and there. I went into the house and got my packboard and 30-40 rifle, and took off across the bridge and down the trail about a mile, to Porcupine Creek. When I began to climb the first one thousand feet, which was on about a half pitch slope, the going was good. I started to follow the hogback, or ridge, where there was a little trail that had been made by goats and bears traveling it for years. This was pretty steep, and on the north side it was almost straight down to the water of Turnagain Arm.

Charlie Mathison had seen the goat on the mountain and had been watching it through his telescope. When he spotted me going up the ridge after the goat, every once in awhile Charlie would check on my progress. He wanted to watch me make the kill. About twelve o'clock noon I got just about to the top and could see for miles across Turnagain Arm; at all the mountain tops, even north you could see Mt. McKinley and Anchorage, back up Bear Creek, Palmer Creek and a good twenty miles up Resurrection Creek. Boy! I felt like this was about as close to heaven as I would probably ever get.

Charlie had decided he had time to have a quick dinner and then watch me make the kill. I had at that time picked up a goat trail, leading off to the left into the rock pinnacles, where the goat should be. I had lost sight of the goat for the last thirty minutes so was walking very slowly and carefully, watching each step and looking for the goat. All at once I came up over a steep rock and there was the goat fifty feet away, looking up Resurrection Valley. It was as still as it could ever be. I could hear my heart pounding. This goat looked like he owned the whole world. What a beautiful sight.

I took aim at his head and pulled the trigger. With a big roar from my rifle I broke the stillness, and I had missed. The goat turned his head to see where the noise had come from. When I pulled the trigger the second time I had a good side shot. He fell off the pinnacle about thirty feet down, onto a shale rock slide; kicked one kick; and slid down the steep shale slide, about two hundred feet, dead as a doornail.

Charlie had too big a dinner I guess, anyhow, he told me later he missed seeing the kill. I had to go back the way I came to get on a better spot to jump down about ten feet on-to this shale slide, and go sliding down to the goat. I dressed the goat out and took its hide off right there. I put its tongue, liver and heart into a flour sack which I always took with me on hunts. I also took part of the skull and horns which I still have on my wall in the entrance way after all these years.

I had a pretty good pack load with all this goat, etc.; around seventy-five or eighty pounds. On my way back down the mountain I had to stop and rest quite often. My legs and ankles were sure aching when I got down to the bridge about four o'clock.

As I came across the bridge I ran into Bill Logman, an old timer who had sold his placer mine in the early days and was now living in a nice log cabin as a retired gentleman. He and Doc Nearhouse were talking when they saw me coming along, so we had to talk about my successful goat hunt. It was great seeing these old boys drooling over this goat and saying how good they were to eat. I asked Doc if after the goat had cooled out a few days, and if I brought a hindquarter over, whether he would cook it for Bill and I. Boy! they were happy as two kids, and sure took me up on that proposition. I hung the goat in my woodshed and went right into the house and laid down for a nice rest (which I had been thinking about for the last two hours).

The next morning I finished washing my clothes. Then I quartered the goat and took a front quarter and some liver over to Ed's house. I had some of the liver with bacon that morning, and it was delicious. I took a hindquarter over to Doc's cabin, and made arrangements to be there the next day about twelve thirty. When I came over the next day you could sniff some mighty good smelling before you got to Doc's house, where the door was standing open.

He had a one-room cabin about twelve feet by twenty-four feet, with a black bear hide on the floor by the bed. A beautiful big lynx fur with its head mounted, the long tufts of hair still on its ears, made a very attractive wall covering.

Doc got the goat roast out of the oven; with potatoes, onions, carrots and rutabagas all in a big roasting pan done up to a golden brown. With a glass of homemade raspberry wine, and with all this good food, Bill, Doc and I had a wonderful feast. I sat at the table with them for about two hours, eating and listening to their conversations about old times.

The contractor who was working on the schoolhouse had one man besides himself and Ed working. They wanted to get the schoolhouse closed-in before bad weather hit, so Ed got me a job with them as carpenter's helper. Boy! I was glad to work with them for about six weeks. I kept busy the rest of the winter cutting wood. I sold wood to Mr. Carson, the Postmaster; George Roll at the store; and Bill Logman. I was making it through the winter in great shape. Joe Richards was going to Seward and asked if I would like to stay in his house for just cutting enough wood to fill his woodshed. I took him up on it, quick, as it was a nice log home with two bedrooms upstairs.

It was the time of winter in Hope when everybody was getting cabin fever, and we men were talking about a dance at the hall. Most all the regular musicians were gone out of town for the winter. We started asking who could play some kind of instrument. Bob Davis and Bob DeFrance were just learning to play the guitar, Louie Shell could play the violin some, and I could play some on the violin left handed. We all got together at my place every night and had a practice session until we thought we were good enough to play for dancing. Louis Shell, son of Mr. Shell, started learning to chord on the guitar also.

We spread around town there was to be a dance Saturday night. Everybody came, happy and raring to get out and have some fun. Gosh! you know we must have done all right with what good old tunes we could play. Everybody danced and had fun. I don't think they went home until one o'clock in the morning. We all looked forward to a dance every Saturday night until spring.

Mrs. Hub Clark (everybody called her Granny) cooked a big turkey dinner for her oldest son, Earl. It was his birthday; and two other old timers, Sam Gates and Elmer Carson (the Postmaster) all had their birthdays in a row. Sam's Feb. 12th, Earl's Feb. 13th, Elmer's Feb. 14th, and somehow they found out mine was Feb. 15th, so I had the pleasure of being invited for the birthday dinner, too. The younger son, Carl, and his wife Emma, were also invited. I am telling you, no words can express my enjoyment at that dinner. I know I ate like a hungry wolf, but never in my life did I ever se a man eat so much and enjoy food like Hub Clark. He had turkey gravy and grease from ear to ear. It just made you enjoy the dinner more to see him eat. Hub had a saying that always tickled me; it was "Dad Blabb it" or "Dad Blabb that".

There was a little log house that Mr. Galligar had lived in, but he had died. It was run down, the floor had rotted out and·a little bush of some sort grew up through a hole in the floor. The cabin had been built by an Indian in 1914. The corners were all dovetailed. It had a ladder up to the bedroom. There was a small kitchen, and porch, and it looked like I could make a livable home out of it. The lot was big with some nice spruce and birch trees. I asked Mr. Nearhouse for the address of the heirs of Galligar's estate, and wrote them asking what they would take for the cabin. They finally wrote back in the early spring that they would take three hundred and ninety-five dollars for it. I got a

Dennie McCart and Louis Shell.

My Log Cabin in Hope

money order made out and sent it to them, and advised them how to make out the deed. Joe Richard's wife was coming home for the summer so I had to move. I showed Doc the letter and moved into the Galliger cabin.

The school was finished and they had some Celotex, ship-lap moldings and other pieces of lumber left over that they did not want to ship back to Juneau. I bought it at a good price and asked Ed if he would do some fixing up and re-pairing on my house. He was glad to get the work.

Early that spring, one Saturday night at the Social Hall, we all decided it would be a fun idea if each family took a turn writing a scandal sheet about everybody or anything happening in the town. Then someone would read it to all the rest of the people at the hall. We sure got some dandies, and I did not get to keep them all, but I was lucky enough to get one Kent King had written in poem form.

He lived on a homestead about one and a half miles out of Hope, and worked on the road. He was going "outside", a saying used when you went to the U.S. for a trip. This was his scandal sheet that he wrote about the people of Hope before he left on his trip.

Come gather around me you people of Hope
If you listen real close I'll give you the dope.
Now, there is Mr. Carson, who handles our mail
If you get into trouble he'll sure go your bail.
There is Hub Clark who has a saw mill
He works very hard and he saws lumber swell.
He has two boys, Carl and Earl
One married a nurse and had two fine baby girls.
Then there is Mr. Davis, Oh! he is so big,
For breakfast he eats the whole side of a pig.
While Mitchell and Brenner raise garden for luck,
Ed Haun and Denny ride around in a truck.
Bob DeFrance sure likes to hunt moose,
While Jim DeRock with a gun on his shoulder
    tramps around through the spruce.
Yes, Iver Nearhouse is a very fine man,

Like all sourdoughs lives out of a can.
  Now Father Devine is new to this clime,
And he seems to be having one hell of a time.
  While working outside in the cold winter fog,
He was badly chewed by a big Husky dog.
  Erve Rheigans is a trapper of considerable note,
He says, "These coyotes sure get my goat."
  Homer Boe goes to the store to buy sauerkraut,
Says George Roll, "Of that I'm just out."
  There is Jimmy Mays, who has a fine little wife,
Who he promised to love and cherish thru life.
  Oh! yes, there is Dryer, the man with long hair,
If he was seen in the brush he'd be shot for a bear.
  Al Ferrin and Swank went out to hunt bear,
When they reported back there was nothing there.
  Tom Sobel says, "I'm a sure shot.
When my rifle goes 'bang' it means meat in the pot."
  Mr. Bixler—I hear—is a "500" fan,
You'll have to watch close for he'll beat you if he can.
  Now things here will be moving,
A rich strike has been found.
  The Buzzard brothers have staked it
Three feet off of the ground.
  Miss Blanc soon will be going,
To the sunny south land.
  Poor Jake not so well pleased
For her cooking was grand.
  Do you know what Joe Richards is telling around?
He says, "My wife is the shortest lady in town."
  And Louie Shell said to me as he filed on a saw
"It looks like I'd have a new son-in-law."
  Old Slim says that Pete is a very good boss
He makes a pal for a very fine hoss.
  Now there is Eddie Swanson who used to fish,
But now the B.P.R. is his main dish.
  The King has gone South, and has discarded his wool.
But leaves Bob Saxton behind, to take care of the bull.
  So now I'll be saying to my friends here at Hope;

"If you get your desserts, you'll be hanged with a rope."

Kent King

There always seems to be something to do those long winter nights. I was starting to court Louie Shell's oldest daughter Flora. I would go over to Joe Richards' to visit before they moved to Seward. He was married to a short Tyonic Indian lady, a wonderful cook. I could always get some tea and cookies and cake which I enjoyed very much as I had a liking for sweets.

5
The Old Time Stories

Joe Richards was a good talker and told me some of the old time stories about the earlier days in Hope, which I will pass along to you.

Around 1917 there was a lot of men living in Hope for the winter. In fact, one winter there were around two thousand people living there in tents. One bachelor had a cow that wandered all over town but was not milking just then. He asked his neighbor to look after her while he went about fourteen miles up Resurrection Creek to see if he could kill a moose.

About a day before he was to return, three or four of the boys decided it would be fun to paint his cow. Well, they painted big red circles around the eyes, green stripes and white spots all over her body. Oh Boy! what a sight. Then they decided it would be fun to put the cow in his one-room cabin and shut the door. It was the next day when he got home. What a mess when he opened the door and the cow came running out. The colors scared him silly. Inside was cow manure, pots and pans scattered, his bed messed up, the stove pipe knocked down and stove upset. Was he ever mad. Nobody ever told him who did it. The old cow lost some hair that spring from the paint job.

One fall they were lucky enough to get a nice looking single schoolmarm to teach school. Of course, it was a challenge right away with all the men to see who would be her beau. There was one fellow, very good looking, but very shy, who wanted to make an impression with her. He went down to Roll's store and bought some chocolate candy. He made the mistake of asking his friends how to go about giving it to her. His friend was very obliging and said, "You write a note asking for a date and sign your name, and I will

22

give it to her." Boy! he fell for that and left the box of candy to be delivered, but before his friend delivered the candy he let the other men around in on the joke he had made up. Well they wound up eating the candy and then filling the box up with horse manure, wrapping it up and giving it to the schoolmarm. There was a good fight or two over that and a lot of explaining to the schoolmarm before things got back to normal.

Charlie Mathison was another person who enjoyed telling about old times. Charlie had a saying instead of swearing; he would use the words "Gosh Ding it". His brother Bob had an expression when talking about something small as a "little bittie teeney weenie thing".

When they were young and had moved to Hope from Texas their Dad started mining on a pretty big scale with a hydraulic plant. His oldest son, John, was a young man with lots of foresight. When they got enough money ahead from mining he bought a steam shovel and started to dig a big ditch up on the bench on Resurrection Creek. This would be about four miles long bringing the water down the ditch. Then they could pipe it off the hill and have a lot of pressure and plenty of water to mine with. He got about one-half mile of ditch dug when he took sick and before they got him to the doctor his appendix burst and he died. The steam shovel stood up there for some time before it was finally brought down and the ditch project was abandoned.

One winter when they were staying downtown, Mr. and Mrs. Mathison ordered from Sears & Roebuck a fancy new cook stove. When it arrived a big gang of people went down to help them set it up. They started a fire in it and everybody was talking about how nice it looked and how hot it was getting on top. The old stove had lots of holes and cracks in it and Mr. and Mrs. Mathison both chewed tobacco so they had no problem finding a hole to spit in. They had plenty of practice so they could hit their special hole dead center. This new stove had Pa getting pretty desperate for a good old spit, until he noticed the draft opening on the side of the new stove which he opened and let go. Well,

Mrs. Mathison took a shot at it right after Pa and before the neighbors left they had the stove well spattered with tobacco juice.

That winter they had a tame one-year-old brown bear, and he would pull a sled, hauling wood. One day some sled dogs got loose and started chasing him, and the bear tried to climb up a spruce tree with the sled tied to him, trying to get away, as the dogs were really after that bear.

The next spring the bear was getting big and kind of mean. Mrs. White, a big fat lady, took care of him. He was tied by a chain on a wire that ran from their house to the old-fashioned outhouse. Nathan White, her husband, was gone on the mail boat trip. She went out to the toilet and was ready to come back in. When she started out of the door the brown bear made a lunge at her and slapped the door, slamming it shut just as she got back inside. Well, she sat there for about fifteen minutes before some men came walking up the street heading for the pool hall. She could see them through the cracks between the boards so she hollered for them to come and chase the bear away from the door. They stopped, looked all around and couldn't see anybody so went on down to the pool hall. After about thirty minutes of sitting and peeking out of the door she saw the bear was far enough from the door so she got out and ran away from the bear's reach. She was so mad that she went into the cabin, got the shotgun and killed the bear. Those men in the pool hall came out in a hurry with a surprised look on their faces. You can see why I enjoyed visiting with these old timers; they were wonderful people.

In the spring everybody was getting cabin fever. That's when the people get crabby at each other and don't speak very much. They would use the expression that "they missed too many boats". It was time to take a trip to Seward for one night, see a ship and talk to other people. That generally did the trick, otherwise nobody ever went seventy-five miles to Seward. Some of the people had been in Hope four years without going to Moose Pass, forty-five miles away.

Nate White and Brown Bear in Hope May 1917. Donated by Mr. and Mrs. Carl Clark.

6
Beginning of the Hope Truck Line

It was the middle of April. Williams and Bill Colb, who had been running a bus and light freight haul from Hope to Seward, were having some breakdowns and a bad time on the roads with the spring breakup. They decided to give the bus and freight hauling up.

I was down at the store getting some grub and Mr. Roll told me about Bill giving up the bus and freight line. He had two tons of freight coming into Seward by steamship and was wondering how he would get it trucked to Hope. I asked whether he would pay a hundred to have his freight hauled. At that time he was paying one dollar per hundred. I asked if I bought a truck if I could have his hauling. He was very excited and said, "Yes". I went over and talked to Bill Colb and Williams, to be sure they had given up the business and they said, "Yes", and there would be no hard feelings towards me taking over the run from Hope to Seward.

I got a ride to Seward with George Brendal who had a Model A coupe. When I got to Seward I started looking around for a used truck. There was a 1931 Model A, one and a half ton long wheel base, for sale with lots of miles on it. The garage man said the engine had just been overhauled and he would let me have it for five hundred and fifty dollars. He would do some work on the brakes and put on a new tire. The other tires were pretty well worn also. I made a deal with him with three hundred dollars cash down and to pay the two hundred fifty dollars balance in two months. Right then and there I had a truck and was in business for myself.

I went down to the dock and picked up the freight for George Roll. It took almost every cent I had to pay the

26

steamship freight bill. I bought gas on time at the garage where I bought the truck. I started for Hope, seventy-five miles away, over a crooked gravel road with two summits to go over, with the most beautiful scenery in the world. Man, I was flying on a cloud. When I got to Hope that evening with George Roll's freight he was a happy man and within an hour everybody in Hope knew I had started a truck line which I would call "The Hope Truck Line".

I was courting Flora Shell at that time and on Sunday morning about ten o'clock I got her in my Model A truck and went for a drive to show off my new purchase. I was pretty proud of this truck. When we got up on the hill just out of Hope I stopped and slid over with my arms around Flora; we were doing some kissing and gazing into each other's eyes like two sick pups. We must have been sitting there in the middle of the road for ten minutes; time flies when you are involved in such important things. All at once out of the corner of my eye I saw a car behind us. There was Mr. Schofield, his wife, and three boys, laughing fit to kill. We jumped apart like we had been hit by lightning and I pulled over into a turnout and let them by. We both were blushing like all get out when they passed waving and laughing. It sure was not long after Schofield got back into Hope that the kids had told all about us smooching in the middle of the road. I could have parked in the middle of the road a hundred times again and never seen anyone, but they caught us that time.

On my trip into Seward I came upon an old fellow with a little packsack on his back walking toward Moose Pass. I stopped and asked him to get in and ride. He looked at me kind of surprised and skeptical. He said, "It all depends on you. You asked me to ride and if you are not going to charge me I'll take you up on the offer."

I said, "You old Coot, you get in here. I wouldn't think of charging you." Right then and there I had another customer, when he needed any freight and groceries hauled. I also had all the other old prospectors hauling. I don't know how the news got around so fast but the old saying "Mukluk

Telegraph" did miracles, and traveled from cabin to cabin like lightning.

When I got to Seward and stopped to pay my gas bill and also get my tires and have the brakes fixed, I got bad news. The garage was closing. The fellow had gone broke. He had turned my note over to the bank. For the work he had promised to do on the truck he gave me an old 2-door Overland sedan and part of another Overland car to use for spare parts. I took him up on the deal and said I would be in Monday with Ed Haun to get the sedan that ran, and haul the other junker to Hope.

I had some groceries to pick up at Brown & Hawkins store for George Roll and a few things for some of the people at Hope. Mr. Hawkins was very nice and seemed to be very interested in me and my venture into running a truck line (which you will hear more about in this book). After I got to Hope and delivered the freight, I was talking to Ed and he said he liked the car and would take it for the money I owed him for doing carpentry work on my house.

The car only had about twenty thousand miles on it and turned out to be a good car. Ed made a good wood saw out of the other motor from the old junker. I told Ed I would be running the truck line and would pay a man one hundred fifty dollars a month to work in my place at the mine so we could see how the ground turned out. If we wanted to keep on mining I would make other plans which Ed agreed to.

The last of May I got a job hauling hand-hewn hemlock railroad ties from Mile 52 on the summit to The Alaska Railroad section house in Moose Pass. It was a twenty-two mile haul, and with the frost going out of the road I got a lot of experience dodging frost heaves and mud holes to keep from getting stuck. I will say the men who tried to keep the road open for my hauling were very cooperative and worked hard.

There was one afternoon when Slim and I were loading ties, we heard a far-away roar and looked across Canyon Creek, and there came a big snowslide off the mountain. A big comber on top of the mountain had let go. Oh Boy!

what a sight it was. The slide was about four hundred feet wide coming down a steep mountain one-half mile from us. It made a very strong wind, fine snow even hit us from that distance. That is the biggest and best snowslide I ever got to see in the daytime.

Around the last of May on one of my trips to Seward, Mr. Swetman, the druggist, introduced me to Dorothy and Jim Shobe who had just arrived in Seward from California. They were waiting for me to move them out to a homestead about four miles up Resurrection Creek from Hope. This was known as the old Koon homestead where Koon had been raising mink in the early days but had never improved on the property. The Shobes applied for the homestead rights. They had about 800 feet of nice cedar lumber, some 2x4, and windows to pick up at Cal Brosius' lumberyard; and a big order of groceries, an axe, bucksaw, etc., to pick up at the Brown & Hawkins store. You could get everything at this store as they had hardware, groceries and clothing all together under one big roof.

We got to the Koon homestead about six o'clock in the evening. There was an old mink house about ten by twenty feet in pretty bad shape, also an old log barn with a sod roof on the place. I got stopped and Dorothy was out of the truck looking for the broom and went into the old mink house sweeping cobwebs, mink and porcupine manure out the door while Jim and I were unloading the truck. I told them they would find water back by the hill about three hundred yards from the mink house. I wished them well with their pioneer spirit, and told them to let me know if I could do anything to help them. Mrs. Alice Mitchell, that lived next to me in Hope, would also be a good person to get acquainted with. I said "goodbye" and drove away. After seeing Dorothy dig in so soon to clean up and get a place suitable to sleep that night I figured they would do all right as homesteaders. Alaska needed people like them.

In June I had a job hauling coal from Moose Pass to Hope where Charlie Mathison, Erv Rheingans, Ken Hinchy and Joe Richards were mining. They were using the steam shovel which John got to build a ditch with years before. I was pretty busy every once in awhile shoveling a carload of coal on and off. One time Ed heard where he could get a winch at Moose Pass for a few dollars. This winch had been taken off of an old '30 gas Caterpillar. We loaded the winch on the back of my load of coal and started for Hope. At Beaver Creek about twenty miles from Hope I came around a sharp corner and there was the Forest Service coming with a Dodge flatbed truck. It was a one-way road and the Forest Service had the inside. He went into the ditch right up against the bank and stopped. I turned out just enough to miss him by a hair but there was not enough road. I went over the bank with a slow roll up on my side against the brush. About a ton of coal rolled off and the winch went out through the brush. After getting out and looking things over, the Forest Service hooked a chain on my truck and pulled it down on its wheels and back on the road. With only a bent fender and some scratches on the door we were OK and thanked the Lord it was no worse. Ed and I had a big job packing most of the coal back up to the road and loading it. It was four days later when I got the winch and took it on to Hope.

I had another close call as I was coming down the hill with a load of coal by Pass Creek. I met George Brendel on a corner. He just swung out and went on by me going plenty fast. I had no way of stopping suddenly with the kind of brakes a Model A had in those days. I think I had my outside dual tires over the bank but we made it. At that spot it was fifty feet straight down to the creek.

I had a job moving four big long timbers at Mile 60 from a dredge, which was being dismantled, for Bob and Charlie Mathison. They were going to build a power barge and needed those timbers. I borrowed a dual-tired trailer from the boys who worked on the road. They didn't make a practice of loaning government equipment but I did them a few favors and they just returned it without anybody saying anything. On a one-way road it was a job getting around some of the sharp curves and turns with this kind of a load.

We had to cut some trees and brush along the road where these long timbers swung out on the turns, but by going slow and careful we made it in one day. I was getting more confident in my truck driving by now.

One morning about five o'clock when I got up the birds were singing their morning songs. I could hear Resurrection Creek murmuring. The sun was just coming up over Bear Creek mountain. It was a wonderful day. I was to be up Palmer Creek at Swetman's mine at six thirty to haul two loads of high grade gold ore up to the Hershey Mine Stamp Mill which stood at the end of Palmer Creek road. I slipped out of Hope that morning while everybody was sleeping, except a few dogs. I spotted a marten crossing the road about two miles up the hill. When I got around Palmer Creek point there stood a mountain goat in the middle of the road. Well, I just floorboarded the gas pedal and was chasing this old billy goat about twenty-eight miles an hour down the road. He was jumping stiff legged with his head up and eyes rolled back. Boy! I was gaining on him when all of a sudden he jumped to one side into the ditch. By the time I stopped he had taken off up the mountain ridge and it was no time at all until he was out of sight. By the time I got up to where the sacks of ore were, I had also seen a moose. I had plenty to tell the men who helped me load the ore. The sacks weighed about one hundred pounds each so it was hard work.

We got to the Hershey Mill just in time for breakfast. Dave Andrews was the cook and had cooked for years in mining camps. When I sank my teeth into his sourdough hot cakes made with graham flour, plate size and about one-half inch thick, Man! Oh, Man! they were good. He could have held a job at the Waldorf Hotel as a cook. That was a breakfast I will never forget. After breakfast we hauled one more load and then I went to Hope.

It was so pretty up near the Hershey mine this time of the year that I asked all the kids and mothers if they could go up Palmer Creek on a picnic the next day. I had a place picked out on a little creek by some snow close to the road. We would take the ice cream freezer along and make ice cream. I also asked Elmer Carson, the Postmaster, to go. He had both legs cut off on account of poor circulation; he took care of the post office in a wheelchair. He was a very independent man but could not refuse an opportunity to get up in the mountains on a picnic. I just picked him up and packed him onto the grass knoll by a small trickling stream beside the snowbank. He just sat there like a sentry on watch for a flock of geese. He noticed every bush, rock and hill. I never saw a person drink in the scenery like he did. We had a wonderful time as I had brought hot dogs to roast and the ladies brought salads and cake plus we had good homemade ice cream.

One day I got a quick request to take Mrs. Joyce Rheingans to the Seward hospital. She was expecting and was getting warnings. We took off in the truck on rough roads with seventy-five miles to go. Whoo-ee! everything went all right until we got over to Jerome Lake and the baby-to-be must have started to complain as Joyce asked me to stop. She got out and walked around some, but in about five minutes she felt OK. Thank Gosh! as I sure didn't want a baby to be born along the road with me as mid-husband instead of an experienced mid-wife. Anyway, we made it to Seward OK. She was happy to have that long ride over with and I was very glad we had made the trip without too much happening. It was almost two weeks later when a nice baby girl was born.

The next day I went up to Mile 60 where the dredge camp was and loaded on an airplane drill which was used for drilling and testing ground for mining. Mr. Stines wanted to see if there was enough gold in the ground to mine down below Cooper Landing by the Skooner Bend bridge. We found my Model A truck was just too small. I was afraid I would upset with that heavy load, or wind up in a canyon, so we unloaded it. They had to get a big truck from the Alaska Transfer in Seward to haul the drill.

I had been a very busy man almost every day fixing something on this old truck to keep it going. I needed a new, bigger truck but I didn't have enough money to buy one.

Pete Ogle had a garage in Seward where I always bought gas. He always stopped any work they were doing to help me fix up the old Model A and get going again. He had shown me a picture of a nice 2-tone flatbed G.M.C. truck with dual rear axle. Boy! I thought it was a dandy but told Pete I could not afford it.

A couple of weeks later I came in on my Friday schedule and the roads were rough. I had generator trouble and the radiator had a hole in it. Oh Boy! was I blue. I pulled up in front of Pete Ogle's garage. I went in and asked Pete if the mechanic could fix my generator while I took off the radiator so they could solder it.

He said, "yes", and we walked across the street to my truck. He was a little short man, always a cigar in his mouth. Right back in the lot from my truck he pointed out a new orange and black truck.

He said, "Come take a look at this." I gloated over it and rubbed the fenders, kicked all the tires, then looked at the springs, etc.

Pete said, "Get in and drive it around the block, the keys are in it. See what you think of it and see how it handles."

I was sure pleased to have the opportunity and jumped right in and drove it uptown a couple of blocks and back. After parking it, I got out and rubbed the seat and fenders some more.

Pete asked me what I thought of it. "Gosh! Pete, it is wonderful. I sure would like to be able to get one like it. Who is it for?"

He chewed on his cigar a little and grinned, then he said, "It is yours."

7
My New Truck

Pete Ogle had written to the Yellow Cab Company in Seattle recommending me and telling about my truck line. We made a deal, Pete would take my truck in for five hundred dollars and what cash I could spare. The Yellow Cab Company would carry the balance. Well, do you believe in miracles? Boy! right then I did. I had tears in my eyes as big as ping pong balls. I shook Pete's hand and thanked him with all my heart. After getting some papers signed and transferring my tools from the old truck to the new one I was still strutting around and looking at the new truck when Pete said, "Get out of here and get to work." Was I ever proud to drive up main street of Seward getting my freight orders and freight at the dock. I could hardly wait for the next day to start back to Hope to show everybody my new truck.

I got a job hauling a little house made of cedar for an artist who was staying in Moose Pass with Ralph Reed. I am not sure of his name but he was a very popular artist painting for magazines, etc. Ralph had recommended I haul the house for him.

Then I got a job hauling five little houses to Skooner Bend just below Cooper Landing for Mr. Stines from the dredge camp at Mile 60. The road to Cooper Landing was a very narrow road with steep hills and pitches so it was a dangerous house hauling job. I had to move along very slow in places, but managed to haul a house each day by putting in long hours.

There was a funny thing happened while I was hauling these houses. When I met someone in a car they would stop and look so lost about what to do on a one-way road and me with the whole road taken up with a house. We always

34

managed to back up or find a place to squeeze by. There were not many cars using the road in those days.

I hired Willie Rheingans, who was fifteen years old, to help me for three dollars a day. He would help with the jacking and blocking when loading and unloading the houses. The first house we took he thought it would be fun to ride in it. I let him climb up into the house and I took off. When I got down on the Cooper Landing road about a mile and had made some steep close turns, all of a sudden I met a car. I stopped to look things over and see where we could pass, also see if the chain binders were tight. Boy! Oh Boy! Willie came out of that house like a scared squirrel. He said when I went around a sharp turn with the house hanging out over the cliff he looked out of the window on the cliff side. It was about forty feet down and the house was leaning on a super curve. He thought he was a goner and got on the other side of the house quick. Anyhow he did not ride in any more houses.

Mr. Stines made arrangements for us to have supper at six o'clock in the evening at Charlie Lean's house in Cooper Landing where Mr. Stines and some of his men were boarding. Mrs. Charlie Lean was a wonderful cook but you would never believe it if you listened to what Charlie said; how he made the biscuits and cooked the chicken just right and his cake being his specialty. His wife just let him carry on with a big smile. We all did our share of laughing and feeling sorry for him. After supper we had to drive back to Hope.

8
Getting Married

After courting Flora for a long time I thought it was about time to get married. This baching and working long hours was for the birds. By then I had my little cabin fixed up like a doll house, with a pump right in the house by the sink, an open stairway up to the upstairs' bedroom; it was cute, I must say. I figured I should be able to get some good looking girl to fall for the house and me.

That spring Flora had a big scare. She was spitting up blood and went to the Seward hospital to see a doctor. They told her she had tuberculosis of the lungs. They gave her a lot of calcium tablets to take which should form a coating around the spot and isolate the problem, and told her to go home and get lots of sunshine and rest.

That summer she gained some weight and was feeling fine so we talked this over pretty well together and figured she had it licked. I asked her to be my wife on September 4th, 1939. She said, "Yes." It was a few days later when we asked her folks. They explained about Flora's illness. They said if it was all right with me, it was all right with them. We set the marriage date for October 23, 1939.

The Reverend Clements, a minister who came to Hope once a month to hold services would marry us in my cabin at two-thirty PM. The bride's sister, Shirley, was bridesmaid. Her brother, Louis, was best man. The bride's father, Louie Shell, gave her away. The Shell family and Ed and Dorothy Swanson were there. Everything went off very smooth considering we had not rehearsed it before. That evening about seven thirty we had a dance at the Social Hall for everybody. They were all to come over to my house later in the evening for refreshments and a piece of wedding cake that Mrs. Shell and Dorothy had baked. About eight thirty I

My Wife Flora.

was playing a few tunes on the violin, Louis was playing the guitar. It was pretty nice of me to let the guys dance with my new wife a few times.

Bob Davis and Bob DeFrance got anxious to get me home for a chivaree or something sneaky. They came up and after putting the violin down they picked me up by the arms and started for the door with me. With a man on each side there was nothing I could do, but as they got to the door I reached out and grabbed each side of the door jamb and put a foot in the back of each man and shoved them on out the door without me. I just turned around and came walking back in the hall like nothing had happened. About then the two Bobs came in to get me, but Boy, Oh Boy! by then Flora had figured out what was taking place and bounced out in front of those guys, starting to tell them plenty. They stopped right then and there. Things calmed down and I asked the two Bobs to play a good waltz for us and we would go home. Flora and I had our dance and scampered home.

We hardly got the fire started in the cook stove, to make coffee and tea when all hell broke loose outside; rifles going off, people hollering and banging on tin cans. After about ten minutes of that we opened the door and asked all the people in. I went up Palmer Creek and got some ice at a snow slide so I had a big tub full of beer on ice sitting on the back porch. Everybody was having a good time when Louis said he thought the beer was going awful fast. He was right. I caught the three Schofield boys grabbing a bottle or two every once in a while and running outside to drink and cash it. I brought it into the kitchen where we could keep an eye on it but the boys had gotten enough to be good and sick the next day. About midnight everybody left and we started those awkward, shy, embarrassing moments of getting into bed.

At eight o'clock Flora was up and ready to cook my first breakfast as soon as I got the cookstove fire going. We just sat around all day looking at the nice gifts people had given us and put things away in the closet. It was just a lovely day to start out our married life. Mom and Pop Shell came over for about an hour, otherwise everybody left the honeymooners alone.

Four weeks later Flora and Dorothy went with me on my scheduled trip to Seward. There was snow on the ground in Seward the next morning. I had a big load of lumber and groceries to load, and got a late start. It was about 2 PM when I left Seward and I got five miles out of town when around the corner came Joe Vonna in Bill Estes Ford pickup going about fifty miles per hour. I turned out as there was plenty of room to pass but he froze to the brakes and came sliding down the road sideways. The back end of the pickup hit my front bumper and fender, swung around like a hammer, and the front of the pickup hit my dual rear tires, knocking that side of my axle loose and cutting a tire in half. The drive shaft was also pulled apart. Damn! a new truck all banged up. It would not have been so bad if I had done it myself. He was pretty well under the influence of booze, and had no money. He would do anything to make it right. In those days anything like that was just settled by the two parties involved. I made an agreement with him, as I was insured, if he would pay the one hundred fifty dollars deductable I would let the insurance company pay the rest. We shook hands which in those days was a binding agreement and I sent word into Seward to Pete Ogle to come and tow me in. Pete and his mechanic, Bill Colb, worked all night to get the truck fixed up. By 8 AM I was on my way to Hope minus one fender but otherwise in pretty good shape. Joe Vonna is dead now but he never did pay me the one hundred fifty dollars which I had to pay out of my own pocket. I don't know how much Pete Ogle's bill was but I want to thank the insurance company for paying the bill as I sure didn't have much money right then after just getting married.

A few weeks after that episode I had got my truck fender on and felt like my truck had a new look.

That morning Flora and Dorothy were with me on my Friday trip. It was raining and the roads were very icy. I had chained up my rear duals but as I came down a hill on a curve about a mile out of Hope I started to slide, and sure enough, wound up over a five-foot bank. The truck ended up on its side. I had about twenty-five empty oil barrels on, which made a lot of noise. About half of them rolled off. The two girls were excited and tried to push the truck door up to get out. They didn't realize I was on the bottom getting tromped by four feet, and Dorothy had pretty high heels on too. We got out and just got ourselves together when Roy Mitchell came by on his way into Hope to get some cinders to put on the road. He said the road was very slick and he had an old chain at the road department that he would give me to put on my front wheel. He would have to get a load of cinders on his truck to be able to pull my truck over on its wheels and back up on the road. He took us back to Hope and I helped him load up with cinders. We did not have any trouble getting my truck on its wheels and back on the road. Very little damage was done to the truck, just got the new fender dented and scratched a little. I remarked to Mitchell the first thing I should do when I got a new truck was to kick the fenders and dent them up some, then maybe I would not have to do it the hard way.

The women stayed home that day. I was almost eight hours getting to Seward. I had stopped to pull other people back on the road and it seemed like I was in every ditch between Hope and Seward. Boy! I got a good lesson in driving on ice and was sure happy to go to bed at the Overland Hotel and try to get some sleep.

Flora and I went for walks up the trail going to the mines on Resurrection Creek. The snow was so pretty and we enjoyed the stillness and fresh air. We would stop once in awhile and have a kiss or two and do some hugging. We got teased plenty the first time we saw Carl Clark and Pete Sorenson. Carl, being a trapper, looked our tracks over in the snow and could see every place we stopped, with my foot tracks pointed towards Flora's foot tracks so close together. Ha! Boy! they had a good laugh, and we did too, but we tried not to make such obvious tracks in the snow after that.

Emma Clark had ordered a washing machine from Sears and I delivered it. With two little girls and lots of washing it was going to be heaven after all the years of washing on an old fashioned wood washboard. The next day Carl came over and told me the gas washing machine had stopped about ten minutes after Emma had started washing and they could never get it started again so she had to wash by hand again. She was sure downhearted and just sick.

I went over and checked it out and the gas motor didn't have a bit of spark. I took the motor off, took it home and started taking it apart to see what was wrong. When the motor got good and warm for the first time it had melted some wax off the insulation on the spark plug wire. The wax fell onto the flywheel covering the magnets that make the spark as the wheel rotates. I took some fine sandpaper and gas and cleaned the flywheel up good and put it together. I turned it by hand with the spark plug out and had a very good spark. Then I took it back and bolted it on the washing machine. Emma and Carl were sure it would not run. After about three tries with the foot starter it took off purring like a kitten. I showed Emma how to start the motor, etc. She finally threw the old washboard in the corner of the woodshed after a few months of washing without any trouble.

9

Animals Along Seventy-Five Miles Of Road

In my travels along the seventy-five miles of road there was always some bear, moose, sheep and goats to see. Fourteen miles out of Seward there was a swamp with lily pads and tall swamp grass, and most anytime you went by there you would see a cow moose and calf eating. Sometimes two or three moose. There was a tall spruce tree with a big round ball on top standing by the swamp. Years ago a heavy snow, or eagle's nest, had caused this unusual growth. Mrs. Nellie Lawing had named it the "Highball Tree". On Sheep Mountain at the head of Kenai Lake, every once in awhile, I would see sheep and bear. Then around Lawing, on a birch flat in the wintertime, you would see five or six moose. Tern Lake was another good spot to see moose and on the high mountain was always bear and sheep. For about eight miles along upper and lower Summit Lake there were lots of moose and sheep on the mountains. From about Mile 49 on, there were goats to be seen in the fall and spring, in the meadows on the mountain two thousand feet up. Beaver Creek was also a good place to see moose.

Oh! speaking of beaver, there were lots of ponds with beaver houses made of sticks and mud rising about five feet above the water. One day I met a beaver coming down the gravel road. He probably got kicked out of the pond he had been living in as they kept their families down to the amount of food around the pond. He was so foot-sore from walking on the gravel that he just sat up holding his bleeding paws asking me to help him. I drove him around the corner over to a small stream where he jumped in with a slap of his tail saying thanks.

One time I came across some little lynx kittens that were sure cute. After looking around closely in the woods I spotted mother lynx so went on my way but was so happy to see them.

At Mile 50 I was on a long straight stretch of road when a coyote jumped out and took off up the road trying to outrun me. I floorboarded the throttle and gained on it and finally ran over it. His head got under the rear dual wheel and with a heavy load I mashed its head flat on the road. I took it home and skinned it out, and a few weeks later I collected five dollars. The Territory of Alaska was paying bounty on them at that time.

In the winter, practically in the same spot, I ran over a wolverine with my pickup. There was a thud and I stopped to pick him up, but no luck. He must have been in the middle of the road and just got hit by the under part of the car. He was picking himself up and growling and took off across the country at a fast run. I bet he thought that was a rough fight. For their size they are one of the toughest, meanest and vicious animals.

I was coming along the road one night in the fall about 8 PM at Mile 64. The moose were rutting and were on the prod. I picked one up in the headlights so I came to a quick stop; there he stood broadside in the road. Oh! what a beauty. I blew my loud trumpet horn thinking I would scare him off the road. No luck; he turned towards me and with my headlights shining in his eyes he was blinded. Within a flash he had let his big 5-foot rack of horns down and charged. Through the windshield all I could see coming at me was these horns. So real quick I leaned on the horn and lay down in the truck seat. Evidently when the bull got up close and could see what he was charging he couldn't stop so just jumped up along the side of my truck. I heard glass and some rattling noises. The truck shook a little. The moose let out a big grunt and I looked out my door window just in time to see this big bull moose pick himself up out of the ditch then take off through the brush. He had lost a fight and was leaving.

After about a minute of getting my wits about me I got out and threw the side mirror off the road which he had knocked off the truck, and Yep! that same front fender mashed down on my tire with a moose footprint in it. My headlight was also knocked out so I threw the glass in the brush. I got a tire iron and jack, pushed my fender up off the tire and went on home. I had some pretty close calls with moose after that but never that bad.

One time I chased a goat for about three miles down the road just before I got to Ptarmigan Creek. Another time I stopped and watched two sheep on a gravel bar at Ptarmigan Creek. They are beautiful animals and I enjoyed watching them for a good ten minutes before they went up the creek bank into the brush. I have eaten mountain sheep and it is delicious.

I took a job hauling a house from lower Summit Lake to Moose Pass. It was sitting up on the bank close to the road. I took the job pretty cheap as I figured it would be easy to slide onto the truck but it was freezing in that country and I found out the house was frozen in the gravel and mud. I picked, shoveled, pried and jacked all day and still didn't get it loose. After driving back to Hope for the night I got an early start the next morning and about 10 AM I got the house loose. Boy! the frost sure can hold onto things. I was very happy when I got the house into Moose Pass for the Wolf family. I sure didn't make any money on that hauling job.

In the wintertime along Kenai Lake road, on what they called "the missing link", glaciers would form from the water coming down the hillside onto the road. I had to get out with axe, pick and shovel to make trenches for my wheels. The road was along the hillside about two hundred feet above the Alaska Railroad almost straight down and I was not about to take any chances. With two trenches as wide as my wheels I could cross without sliding off. The road men could always tell if I had been through during the night by the trenches in the ice.

In the winter before the missing link was finished they drove over Kenai Lake on the ice, from Lawing to Mile 18, and it was pretty risky business. You had to look out for air pockets and every once in awhile you would hear the ice crack from pressure, with a big bang. The sound would go off down the ice like a rifle should in the distance. This was pretty scary when you were a half mile from shore and it was four miles across to Mile 18 from Lawing. In the early days a team of horses with a sled load of freight fell through the ice and drowned. The driver got on safe ice and survived. In the summer they used a small boat and barge to haul people and freight from Mile 18 to Lawing, otherwise you used the railroad. So it was a happy day when the road was built and people could travel to Seward any time by car.

The winter of 1940 Cal Dryer and Joe Richards hewed railroad ties for the Alaska Railroad. This is a hard job. The ties are made from hemlock trees about a foot in diameter at the stump and hold that size for about twenty-five feet. If all goes well they will get four to five ties from a tree. You use a big broad axe which has a blade ten inches wide and weighs six pounds. You stand on the log and hew two sides with a six to eight inch flat surface, then knock the bark off the remaining parts. The ties are eight feet long and heavy. These old tie hackers can hew a tie so smooth with an axe that you would think they had planed it by hand. I had the job of hauling the ties to Moose Pass to the railroad siding for them.

That early fall at the Hope Social Hall they stopped the dance and Pop Brenner came out into the middle of the hall with an umbrella turned upside down and announced they were going to have a shower. Well, I thought Gee! one of the women was expecting, and when Mr. Brenner looked over at Flora and I, Boy! I was puzzled. Everybody came out and put packages into the umbrella and then Mr. Brenner gave a speech on how all the people of Hope appreciated all the little errands and extra things Dennie did for them and this was their way of saying "thanks". Flora and I were kind of choked up and I don't even know what I said outside of "thanks" and we were so happy to think of them all as our big family.

10
The Winter Moose Hunt

Just before Christmas everybody that had a dog team went up Resurrection Creek on a moose hunt. It was about 12 miles up to Fox Creek where there was a cabin and a good moose hunting area. There was lots of swampy willow country and open rolling hills. Ed and I had no dogs so made plans to take some food and sleeping bags and hike five miles up Resurrection Creek to O.T. Hill and stay in Leo Sears' cabin. We would do some hunting on snowshoes on the hill above the cabin. We got to the cabin about 10 AM and left our belongings, then took a sandwich with us and went up on the hill. It was not long after we got up there until we picked up a moose trail going along the ditch line back towards Hope. We started following the tracks thinking this is great going right back to Hope would mean less miles to pack the meat. We followed those tracks down almost to Hope and then the tracks took off up the mountain. We were not about to follow any farther as it was late in the afternoon and we were tired so we came off the hill into Hope. Ed and I figured the boys with the dog teams knew where to go get the moose and had better transportation. I would go up early the next day and get our belongings that we left. I got there about 10 AM and thought I would go up on the hill into Gold Gulch and take a look for moose before going back to Hope. It was easy snowshoeing in our tracks from the day before. Just as I started into the valley of Gold Gulch two moose jumped up only about two hundred feet from me on the hill in an old burned-off area. The sudden surprise caused me to turn, and my snowshoes came off my feet and there I stood in two feet of snow. Right in that position I took aim at the closest moose and killed it with a bang. Then I took a second shot at the second moose for Ed. Darn! I missed so I took another shot and missed again. Oh Boy! I wondered if I had buck fever as they call it. I checked myself to be sure I was aiming at the moose and shot and missed again but saw an old snag break just under the moose's belly. It was starting to go away when I shot my last shot but I got him.

That's when the work started. I dressed out both moose, took a stick and propped one moose open so as to cool out good. I skinned the other moose, quartered it and laid it up on some old snags to cool. Then with the heart, liver and tongue of two moose in my pack I hurried down the hill to the cabin before dark. I got there about 4 PM, grabbed a peanut butter sandwich, loaded up all the belongings on my packboard and started down a good trail for Hope. I must have had about a ninety-pound pack so was walking pretty slow and resting once in awhile and was getting tired.

I was thinking I might have to stay with George Sheppard and Bieswanger at Clark's mining camp four miles from Hope when all at once I heard some dogs.

Carl Clark was at camp and was hooking the dog team up to go to Hope. I started hollering to beat all, and after the third holler with no answer, I was about to give up hopes for a ride the last four miles. The dogs were quiet so I figured Carl had left. Then I heard Carl holler. I was just around a curve in the trail and I hollered to wait for me. Gee! those dogs and that sled looked good to me. Carl put my heavy pack in the sled and I just flopped in with a big sigh of relief and hung on. As soon as Carl told those dogs to go, we were off headed for home. The dogs knew it and sure did travel fast. Carl left me off in front of Ed's cabin and I thanked him and went in and told Ed about the moose. He would not believe me until I showed him the livers, hearts and tongues.

The next day I made a deal with Louis Shell, who had some dogs, to haul the moose down to Hope for half. We went up to get one moose as he only had five dogs. I learned something new right then and there. I was to handle the gee pole. It is about a seven-foot pole sticking out from the front of the sled just about waist high which you used to guide the sled with to keep the sled on the trail. You have the dogs out in front of you with a seven-foot rope from the front of the sled to the first dogs; they are called the wheelers. The rope was called the toe line. The gee-pole man, who was me, had to trot along on snowshoes guiding the sled. Anytime we came to a sharp turn in the trail I had to jump over the toe line so as not to get tangled up in the rope and fall down. After a few miles of practice and almost falling I got the hang of this. Of course, Louis had a few good laughs and we finally got up to the moose kill. We loaded one moose on the sled and started down across a gradual slope along the hillside. Then we had about five hundred feet of steep hillside down through some small spruce with three feet of fine powdery snow. We cut a small spruce tree and tied it on the back of the sled with a dog chain, for a drag, or brake, as the little foot brake on the sled was not efficient in the deep snow. Louis was to stand on the tree for weight. We took off down that hill. The dogs were not about to let a sled pile up on them so they were sure running for their lives with me hanging on to that gee pole with my snowshoes flying like geese taking off the ground. Louis started to laugh at the funny sight and he fell off the drag tree. Oh Boy! I felt the sled lunge forward and I stumbled with my snowshoes. The next thing I knew I was digging the snow out between the sled runners, with the sled, moose and all on top of me. I could see Louis laughing and the dogs sitting in the snow with their tongues out laughing. Louis finally got the sled off and I got the snow brushed from my clothes. We made it on down to the main trail without another pile up. One place along the trail we crossed a little creek where there was ice and a steep little hill to go up. We were pushing, pulling and Louis was hollering at his dogs. Their toenails were digging in and I even saw his lead dog reach out and grab a limb on some brush to help pull with his teeth. Right then and there I could see why the dog mushers speak very highly of their lead dogs. The next day we got the other moose down home without any trouble.

A few days before Christmas the men and dog teams from Fox Creek came home with their sleds loaded with moose meat. Everybody was happy to have enough meat for the winter and we all had lots to be thankful for at Christmas time.

The mail came in with all the things the people ordered from Sears & Roebuck. The people were all wearing something you had never seen them in before. We had a big pot-luck dinner Christmas afternoon and a dance. There was so much food that we all came back the next day to eat again.

The rest of the winter seemed to go by pretty fast with everybody getting their wood in for the summer.

Early one morning in March I was going to Seward to get a load of freight and Mr. Mitchell wanted me to stop at the Moose Pass Highway shop and leave an order with Roy Thurston for some parts and supplies. When I pulled up across the road at the Moose Pass shop about 9:00 AM and started to walk across the road to the shop, Mrs. Harry Smith, who was coming down the road from the Moose Pass store, called to me and wanted to know if I would get two items from Brown & Hawkins store for her. While I was writing this down a big explosion took place at the Highway shop. It sounded like twenty sticks of dynamite. The big window on the side blew out about ten feet, frame and all, the glass was not broken and fell to the ground. The big front door blew out fifteen feet and fell to the ground. A big hole blew in the roof and gray smoke and fire was shooting into the air. Bill Saxton was holding on the wall where the window had been trying to walk out. I ran over. Roy Thurston, Fred Laubscher and Ken Condit were coming out in a daze looking shocked, wondering what happened. Lyle Saxton was helping his dad, so Fred gave Lyle a hand and Bill hobbled out to the dump truck about forty feet away and got up in the seat. Roy and Condit rushed in and got a Dodge pickup and Ford dump truck out before it got so hot they could not go in anymore. I noticed Bill in lots of pain so I told Fred to back the truck that Bill was in over to the roadhouse and get a mattress, and I would back my truck over there and we would put the mattress in the back of my truck for Bill to lay on. By then Lyle, Roy and Ken helped put Bill in the truck. No one else was hurt, except Condit had a cut on his cheek where he had been blown against the wall and scratched by a nail or something. Fred Laubscher and Bill Saxton were in the back of my truck and I looked over at the shop, and black smoke was shooting up through the hole in the roof about one hundred feet with a big red fireball on top. I took off for Seward to the hospital. I stopped once at Mile 18 to see how they were doing. When I got to the back of the Seward hospital we got a stretcher and got Bill into the X-ray room. I told Fred I would get my load of freight and shopping done and pick him up to return to Moose Pass in about one hour. By then we would know how bad Bill was hurt. Bill had a leg broken just below the knee. When we got back to Moose Pass the shop was burned to the ground with the ghostly look of a Cat, bulldozer, Autocar truck with roto snow blade and Ford dump truck loaded with sand all bent and burned to distruction. The men were all alive and not burned but were very stiff and sore for a few days from the concussion. I am so thankful that Mrs. Smith called to me and I missed being in the explosion and fire.

That spring, in April, Flora was not feeling well so I took her to Seward to the hospital. Dr. Banister said she had better stay in there for a month and they would give her treatments and rest. He never did charge me much for all his medical services, but of course I had plenty of bills from the hospital. I was so thankful to have lots of hauling to do that summer and could pay them what I owed. The hospital was very good, they never did say anything when I was behind on paying them.

11
Hauling Freight and Gold

I had a good job for Griesse and Lucky hauling high-grade ore over to the Orical Mine where George Lindsay milled the gold out for them. That same spring George Lindsay hit a rich pocket of gold ore in his mine, and was paying off all his bills he owed stores, lumber yards and everyone he had borrowed from. Some people got money they claimed he owed them that I don't think he ever owed money to in the first place. He and his wife, Bess, went outside to Seattle that fall to spend the winter in a hotel living like king and queen. In the spring they came back with a new pickup. In about a month after returning to the mine the rich vein pinched out and Lindsay was back to a lot of work and no gold.

I also had a bad time that summer hauling two horses to Hope for Kent King. One was very little trouble, but the other one was so spooked and seasick that they could not get him off the ship. When I got to the dock they were wanting to sail but could not get the horse off. I went down into the ship's hold. I could see the horse was just wild from fellows pulling, hitting and trying to get him into a stock crate to be lifted out. The sling man and I put a cargo net under the horse's middle and started taking up slack and hoisted him out. This poor horse's eyes were bulging out and he was breathing so hard his breath was in big snorts. He hung in the net like a limp rag. When they swung him over onto the dock he would not stand on his legs. I had them lift him up and down a few times until he would stand. Then the steamship took off immediately. I drove my truck to where the horse was and tied the horse to the back of the truck. By taking it easy I lead him off the dock and over to a dirt bank where I would load him on my truck. Well, I had made a mistake. I should have loaded him on the truck when the men slung him off the ship as I could not lead him onto the truck. He was on good old ground and he was staying there. I had to get a stock shipping crate from the dock and by putting a looped rope around his body, behind his front legs, with the rope coming up between his front legs and through the halter ring, I snubbed the rope to the truck and started pulling real slow. When he felt that looped rope getting tight around his middle he came into that stock crate in a hurry. Then I walked the other horse on the truck. I was a happy truck driver when I got them to Hope and unloaded at King's ranch. I don't think the one horse ever did get over his steamship ride.

That fall when I was not too busy I stopped at lower Summit Lake and walked three miles up to Slatter's cabin where he was doing some hard-rock mining. Gee! it was a pretty setting. The cabin was hardly weathered being in freezing weather seven months of the year, it was like being in a deep freeze. Off to the east was a big meadow and farther back on the mountain there were forty sheep grazing. I sure did enjoy the view and the hike for a change from truck driving.

Sometimes I would get so tired and road weary that I would get sleepy. That's when it would be time to get out by a mountain stream and wash my face in ice cold water. Boy! that would wake you up and almost made your face numb for awhile. One thing I noticed by lots of the little streams was a tobacco can with a long string on it hanging on a limb of a tree. I inquired from some of the road men about it; they said that was what the old timers used when they went through the country in the winter. While running behind a dogsled they got thirsty. The snow being around six feet deep it was almost impossible to get down to the stream for a drink. They just let the can down and got a drink. The road men continued using the same method and I did too the next winter.

That fall I had a talk with Doctor Banister and told him I had some trouble once with my appendix and that it might be a good idea to have it removed. If I should have an attack and be snowbound in Hope I might not be able to get to a hospital in time and go just like John Mathison did in the early days. Well, he agreed and said he would wait for his money if I could pay the hospital. I hired Mr. Rheingan to run my truck for two weeks and he took us to Seward. I went into the hospital that evening and told the nurse what I was there for. She just laughed and told me to get out of there and quit teasing her. I finally told her to call Doctor Banister as apparently no one had made arrangements for me to be a patient there. When she came back to the waiting room she had a big smile on her face and said, "Come with me. You may not be sick now but just wait until I get through with you." Ha! she was right.

The next morning I was ready for my appendix to be removed. Everything went okay and Flora was talking to me about my operation by 1 PM that same day.

The second day Cal Brosius, who ran the lumberyard in Seward, stopped in at 6 PM for a visit. After visiting me a few minutes, he scolded me for not telling him I was sick then he reached into his back pocket and took out his checkbook and said, "Dennie, how much money do you need?". I kind of stuttered and after a few tears I told him I had enough to pay the hospital; Dr. Banister would wait for his and that it was sure a wonderful feeling to have friends like him. He said he knew I was having lots of hospital bills with Flora's illness and would be happy to loan me some money if I needed it. After he left I just thought about some remarks I had heard from some people around Seward that Cal was a crabby old bachelor. Boy! he was a wonderful old sourdough in my book, and no one had better tell me a bad thing about Cal again.

One time when I was down at the lumberyard picking up some lumber for the Mathison brothers, Cal told me to go up and see "Whispering Suzie"; well, he had to do some explaining about who he was talking about. It turned out to be Lennard, the plumber, and that all the old timers had tied the handle "Whispering Suzie" on him because he had a big loud voice and you could hear him two blocks away. After I had talked to Lennard a few minutes I knew he was well-named by the old timers. While I was there I made some arrangements for hauling some mining equipment.

A few weeks after my operation I got a contract to cut fifteen cords of wood for the school in Hope. I started in on that job kind of slow at first but in a few weeks I was feeling good so all my spare time I worked at that job until I finished in February.

Mr. and Mrs. George Roll did not visit very much with people in Hope but Flora and I asked them over to our house for dinner. They were very happy to accept. The Rolls called everybody by their last name but Flora and I were Mr. and Mrs. Dennie. I kind of liked that as everybody along the road and in Seward called me Dennie. It was not very long after we had the Rolls to dinner and a nice visit that Mrs. Roll invited us to their house for dinner. We had some nice dinner wine and the table was set with the finest of silverware. We enjoyed a good ham dinner and also a nice visit. The place was very plain and they even packed their water from the creek and the house was clean and orderly just like the store.

Later on in the spring I was making a round trip to Seward and Mr. Roll went with me. He bought my dinner at Cameron's restaurant and he visited with Mrs. Cameron, as she knew him for years. Mr. Roll and Mr. Hawkins had a big time talking about store business and old times. Mr. Roll sure did enjoy that trip.

There was snow on the ground when we asked Elmer Carson to our house for dinner. He was always teasing Flora about her cooking. He came the three blocks on a little kid's sled, pushing himself with two short sticks with sharp nails in the ends as he had both legs off. He jumped with his hands into our house when I opened the door just like anyone else would enter. He enjoyed the dinner and we had a good visit. He told about the early 1908 days when all the miners were shoveling by hand on their small claims. He told me about the grave marker which was rounded off on top. He said the man was hijacking or stealing gold out of a sluice box that belonged to another miner. He was shot dead. They held a miners' jury and declared it was just a killing. They took him upon the bench 100 feet from the old Resurrection Creek trail and buried him, and that was that. Later that evening Mr. Carson took off on his own for home, looking at everybody's house as he went by. He had enjoyed a few hours away from the post office.

That spring I got the job hauling all the groceries and freight which came in from Seattle for the St. Louis Mining Company. Before it had always been the Estes Bros. job to haul their freight. I also made a deal with Earl Clark that I would bring out from Seward fresh meat and vegetables every week. When the last mile of road was too muddy to travel by truck, I would park my truck in a turnout at the end of the gravel road and load my packboard with all the vegetables, meat, mail and other little orders for the miners, like gloves, socks, underwear, etc. Sometimes I would have a ninety or one hundred pound pack to put on my back and hike the mile to camp. I got three dollars for this every Sunday morning.

Dorothy Shobe looked out of the homestead window of the little house which they had fixed up so nice after once being a mink house, and wondered how on earth I would ever get to the mine with that big load. Guess that's why my ears are so long, from being a jackass. Ha!

That spring I had the privilege of taking two of Earl Clark's cleanups to the Seward Bank. The gold was in a coffee can and there was around two hundred ounces which amounted to about six thousand dollars in those days. I could just take the coffee can lid off and let the gold sift between my fingers like wheat. Nobody worried about holdups. Who knew what I had anyhow? I just sat it on the floorboard of my truck behind my legs. When I parked in front of the Seward Bank and came walking in with this coffee can, which weighed about nineteen pounds, the banker, Mr. Balderson, knew darn well what I had. I nodded my head to where the big gold scale stood. Mr. Balderson came through a swinging door from the cashiers' area and started to weigh out the gold. It gave me great pleasure to watch him.

When he got down to the last pennyweight or two, he would hold his little finger out and, with the penny weight between his other fingers, drop it on the scale and look up watching to see if the scales would balance. He really enjoyed weighing gold and while doing this he would tip his head and twist his big long black mustache.

That summer whenever I had a day to spare, Flora and I went on lots of drives along Turnagain Arm and up Palmer Creek. We enjoyed seeing the bear, moose and goats on the mountain. Once in awhile all Flora's folks would go with us on a weiner roast along a nice creek. Flora had six sisters and two brothers. I came from a big family also; there was six boys and six girls, so you see I felt right at home with a big family around.

12
Almost Got My Load Froze

It was the last of November when I was going to Hope with a big shipment of canned goods, milk, flour, potatoes, etc. I had arranged my load with the flour and canned meats on the outside of the load; that way the potatoes and milk would not freeze so easy and as long as I was moving the canned goods would not freeze.

I had just got up the hill by Jerome Lake at 6 PM and the temperature was zero. Well, I noticed something different about the road, but my headlights showed the road was okay ahead so I kept going. All at once I was in something just like sand. I could not steer the truck worth a darn and my dual rear wheels started to chomp. There I was, stuck. I got out and looked things over. A snowslide had come down but most of the snow was over by the hill. The snow was real dry and powdery and about a foot of this powdered snow had run over onto the road. It was about two hundred feet across this powdered snow to where it was good going again. I got my scoop shovel out and shoveled the snow from under my truck, then shoveled two paths for the truck wheels about twenty feet out in front. Then I pulled out two big tarps that I always carried along, folded them about two feet wide, and laid them on the snow out from where I had shoveled. I got in and took a run at it and got about sixty feet the first time. I repeated the same thing two more times before I got through the sandy snow and on my way again. I sure worked up a sweat even though it was zero. I was sure lucky nothing froze on that trip. Lyle Saxton told me later about the road men's discussion trying to figure out how I made it over the snow. They knew nobody but Dennie would do that much shoveling to get through a snowslide.

They didn't know about me worrying and sweating it out with a load of groceries about to freeze.

That winter I had a job hauling rainbow-Dolly Varden trout to the Alaska Steamship Company from Lawing every week for about two months. Mr. Plowman had a net at the mouth of Ptarmigan Creek where it ran into Kenai Lake. He would have from one hundred to two hundred nice big trout every week. The old fellow made enough money to see him and his wife through the winter.

13

World War II and Being a Territorial Guard

World War II had broke out and in November 1942, I signed up with the Alaska Territorial Guard. R.C. Mitchell was company commander and there were ten men in our group. We were issued rifles and ammunition and had some training sessions.

That fall I was on my way to Hope when the people at Moose Pass told me the road was closed by a rock slide about two miles out. The road crew was out with trucks and shovels getting the road open. I went on out to the slide. The slide had come from the top of the mountain with water, mud and shale. The road men had been working on it for three hours. It seemed as fast as they scooped it off the road some more oozed out. It was a slimy mess. I walked up past the cars that were waiting to get through. There were four army trucks loaded with soldiers on the other side waiting.

Lyle Saxton got off the shovel and came over and asked me if I had anything to eat on the truck, as they came out without eating before noon and were pretty hungry. I had a nice big cake that the baker in Seward had given me for wrapping one hundred loaves of bread to take out on my route. He was short of help in the bakery so that is why I had to wrap my own bread. I had big hopes of eating this cake at home with Flora and her family. But then I told Lyle I would be right back, and went to the truck and got that nice cake and took it to the men figuring I would share it with them. Lyle motioned for Max Foster, Ken Condit, Fred Laubscher and Roy Thurston to come. When I got back with the cake and they saw it, Boy! Lyle grabbed it and broke off a big chunk and passed it on. After they all got a big chunk they started gobbling it down and handed me the box. Yep! it was empty. I never got a taste of that cake. They all laughed and I am sure they enjoyed every bite of

the cake. Maybe it was more fun for them just to know they
ate it all without me getting a bite. I had to wait about two
hours before I got through that mess. The next spring I got
even with Lyle but it didn't turn out to be such a big laughing matter. I will tell you about it later.

When I came out of Seward on my Saturday trip I was always sure of a cup of tea and cookies when I stopped at
Dominic Kelly's home at Mile 20 to leave off some coal and
groceries. He was a railroad station foreman and he got his
English bride through correspondence. She was a lovely
lady and wanted to know what the news was along the
road. She always had the tea poured and some cookies ready
and there was no way to get away without a little visit while
she paid for the freight.

I had passengers who were riding with me remark that
every house I came out of I was eating and if it was at their
dinner time I would always be offered a piece of chicken or
meat so I faired pretty good.

Well, back to Lyle Saxton. He and his wife, Louise, and
their two boys passed me going to Seward. Lyle had told me
I could do a better job shopping for them than they could. I
did a lot of shopping this particular time and he stopped and
teased me about doing the shopping. Now they were going
to Seward to have fun and live it up. The people never
locked their doors in those days so when I got to his house I
took the grocery order in. I sat down at the kitchen table
and made out the bill. There in the middle of the table was
a nice big cake. I got up and took a plate out of the cup-
board and cut a big piece off and ate it. Then I wrote on the
bottom of the bill, "damn good cake", put the plate in the
sink and went on my way.

I found out later what happened. When Lyle and the
family got home about 6 PM Louise and the boys went in
the house while Lyle put the car in the garage and came in.
He heard Louise scolding the boys in a pretty loud voice and
they were denying the wrong doings so Lyle asked what the
argument was about. Louise jumped on to Lyle then for
taking a piece of cake before dinner as she had been accus-

ing the boys of it and Lyle denied eating any cake too. I guess Louise was pretty mad to think that one of them was lying to her. About then Lyle looked at the bill I had left and saw my smart remark, "damn good cake". He began to laugh like crazy which did not help poor Louise's problem. He finally showed her the bill and explained what happened and the boys thought it was pretty funny too. I am quite sure I was a very unpopular man around Louise's house for a long time. I only hope she has forgiven me by now. I got even with Lyle when it comes to cake eating.

Mrs. Ralph Reed was another dear old lady who lived right in Moose Pass. She and Ralph treated me like a son, and many a time she would give me some homemade chocolate fudge.

Mr. Swetman, the druggist in Seward, always gave me the stripped magazines. These were the ones he did not sell and were out of date. He just returned the front page and got credit for them. I would give them out to the old prospectors and people along the road. I had funny papers and funny books, too, and all the kids looked forward to getting those. It made me a pretty popular guy with everybody.

Mr. Swetman would let any kid in Seward who had no money to buy funnies just take one and sit on the floor behind the counter and read, but they had to be quiet. Sometimes there would be six kids back there. It paid off as no kid would have ever thought of taking anything from that store, and these kids let all the other kids know that they had better not take anything either.

Mr. Swetman joined the Masonic Lodge in Seward and was being initiated, and as part of the initiation the men handcuffed him to the light post down on the street corner. They left him there for awhile and went back up to the lodge hall. They looked out the window a short time after they had left him and noticed he was smoking. They went back down and took his cigarette away from him trying to figure out how he could get a cigarette and light it. Anyhow, they took his cigarettes and matches and went back upstairs. In a little while they looked out and noticed he was smoking again so they took his cigarette away again and this time they watched from the window. What took place was that some of those kids lit a cigarette and put it in Swetman's mouth as they walked by. So you can see Swetman's kids did not let him down.

There were a few times I didn't have enough cash to pay for the freight at the dock. You had to pay the steamship hauling charges before picking up the freight. I would walk in and ask Swetman for a loan. If some people were standing by I would say, "I need four hundred dollars."

Swetman would say, "Okay, ring the cash register and count four hundred dollars out for me." He would throw down the sales book and I would put the date on, mark it "I owe you four hundred dollars", and sign it, take one slip and he would put the other in the till and I was on my way. People could not figure what was going on.

In a few days after I had delivered the freight to the mines and collected I would walk into the drugstore and say, "Mr. Swetman, you poor old devil, do you need four hundred dollars?" People would pick up their ears and I would count out four hundred dollars and give it to him. He would smile, ring the cash register, put the money in and carefully slip me the IOU. I would tear the two slips up and throw them into the wastebasket and go on my way. There were three or four times when he helped me like that.

14

I Got The Mail Contract

I bid on the contract for hauling mail from Seward to Moose Pass. It was the first Star Route ever to be run by motor vehicle in Alaska. Always before it was hauled by boat, dog team or pack horses. Pete Ogle and Mr. Hawkins had seen in the paper that I got the mail contract before I got to Seward. As soon as I got to town and pulled up to get gas, Pete Ogle told me that I got the mail contract. I was all excited and told Pete I would have to go have Bob Baumgardner fix me up a ten thousand dollar bond. Pete grinned and said, "We have it all fixed up Dennie, Mr. Hawkins and I will furnish you a bond. Come on over to Brown and Hawkins store and sign the papers and take the bond up to the post office." I am telling you these businessmen in Seward were special people to help me like that without charging me for the bond.

That winter there was a big snowslide at Boston Bar at Mile 61 and nobody could get through to Seward. I had my mail route to run and there was no way to get word or get to Seward unless I put on snowshoes and started walking to Moose Pass forty-five miles away. Talk about Mukluk Telegraph; Pete Ogle had found out from the road men about the slide and got Charlie Evans to run my mail route. He sent word not to worry he had taken care of it. Of course, being one of the bondsmen he was concerned. It was wonderful of him to keep me from walking on snowshoes to Moose Pass. I paid Charlie for the job well done and told Pete that anytime I did not show up by 2 PM on Friday to have someone haul the mail to Moose Pass for me.

The night the slide came down at Boston Bar I must have just got by when it happened. There was a clear sky and lots of snow on the trees. I just got around a sharp curve one-

63

fourth mile from Boston Bar when all at once I was hit with a strong wind with snow in the air everywhere. I could not see a thing. I stopped real quick wondering if I had run off the road into a snowbank. I got out to see what happened. Everything was quiet. I was on the road but my truck was covered with a fine dry snow about two inches thick. I had to scrape hard with my hands to clear the windshield and get the snow off the headlights. I noticed the snow was off all the trees but I went on and stopped at Erdmans' cabin one-half mile on down the road. I asked Jimmy Newman if he had heard anything. He said, "No, but a strong gust of wind had hit the house about thirty minutes ago." I sat there having tea and a couple of Jimmy's special homemade cookies. They were about five inches across and very good. He said, "I like man-sized cookies, then you don't have to eat so many."

The next day when we learned that there was a big slide at Boston Bar, then I knew what happened the evening before. I just got by in time. A big comber had broken loose on top of the two-thousand-foot mountain and came down and covered the road with dry snow about eighteen inches deep for a good one-fourth mile. At the foot of the mountain the snow was a good sixty feet deep; that is why it created so much wind. This was the slide that kept me from getting to Seward on Friday to run my mail route.

I had talked to the military draft board to see where I stood about being drafted. I was eligible, but they had changed my classification as I was essential to all the people in the community. I had a meeting with the tire allotment board to be sure I could get tires when I needed them. With all this done I just kept busy with all the long hours I could work.

The last year before the war was over I hauled three thousand telephone poles, a lot of piling and freight. I spent many an eighteen-hour day hauling on icy roads. I made good money, but by then it seemed like Flora was in the hospital about half the time so I kind of paid for a hospital or two but was thankful to be able to pay my bills.

Some nights I would come into Seward at 8 PM hungry as a bear. The waitress would just sit and watch me eat wondering where I put all that food. Then for a good sleep at the Seward Hotel.

One day that fall as I started out of Seward with a load of groceries, flour, two mattresses, bales of hay, etc., I was routed to the army base for a search as there was something missing from the dock. It was spitting snow and rain mixed, and the army said they had to check my load. Before I could hardly think, four or five soldiers got up on my truck, removed the tarp and started unloading and pawing through the freight. The mattresses were getting wet and dirty. Oh Boy! I let out a big holler and said whoever the captain or the man in charge was to get Col. Chamberlin on the phone and tell him Dennie McCart of the Hope Truck Line was having inspection in the rain and to please do something about it as my freight was being ruined. When I mentioned the Colonel's name things stopped. Within a few minutes the man in charge came back and gave orders to put everything back as they found it and for me to be on my way with a big apology. That did not make the mattresses dry or clean but Mr. and Mrs. Boe at Hope were glad to get them even though they were soiled.

I will tell you how I got acquainted with Colonel Chamberlin before this occurred so you will understand why I got the order so quick to stop inspection.

One night about seven PM I was on my way to Hope and saw some headlights coming around the curve one-fourth mile from me, and knowing the road like I did, I pulled into a turnout just a little farther down the road as it was a one-way road. Mr. Swetman was a friend of Colonel Chamberlin and asked him to sneak away from the army base and take a ride out to the Hershey gold mine about ninety miles from Seward. He would see some beautiful scenery and get away from army life for a few hours. He accepted so he was along. Swetman said, "I bet you ten dollars that is Dennie coming and he will be sitting in a turnout waiting for me to pass about one-fourth mile from here." The Colonel told

Swetman that nobody knew the road that good and took the bet. When Swetman pulled up to my truck a few minutes later he was laughing and took the Colonel's ten dollars. Then he introduced me to him and we had a little laugh and went on our way. That is why the Colonel knew who I was when they told him about my inspection. I appreciated what he did for me as those soldiers could have ruined my load.

Colonel Chamberlin and Swetman went to the Seward bakery for coffee and doughnuts once in awhile, and one day I came in the bakery to place an order. I sat down over in the corner and ate a sandwich. I didn't think they saw me, but when I went to pay my bill Mrs. Urie said it was paid by a friend. That's all she would say. About two weeks later I saw those two old cronies going to the bakery so I just phoned Mrs. Urie and told her to charge me for Swetman and Colonel Chamberlin's bill. She laughed and said okay. I don't think they every did figure that one out. Ha!

The next spring, in June, when the king salmon were running some of the men in Hope caught some nice big king salmon in their nets, and were sending them into Seward to the meat market to sell. As I came through the last covered bridge on Resurrection River by the army base a military sedan pulled out on the road, and I noticed some Majors and Colonel Chamberlin in the car. With some fast thinking I flagged them down. I got out and went to the side where Colonel Chamberlin was sitting in the back. I said real nice and loud, "Colonel Chamberlin, I have that fish you caught. Do you want it right now, or should I take it over to your office?" I was winking and making signs for him to keep quiet.

I opened the door of the car and let him out. He cleared his throat and stuttered and stammered, and by then I got one of those big salmon out of the pile of grass that was covering the fish. I put it in the back of the car while the rest of the fellows were getting out, asking the Colonel when did he sneak out to get a fish like that. There was a lot of talking going on and the Colonel said goodbye to me with a grin on his face that I will never forget. He was sent to Germany soon after that and we never did get together again to talk about that fishing trip. I bet he had fun with the other fellows though. I heard later on that Colonel Chamberlin was killed in Germany.

I had lots of fun with people along the road but sometimes some of the people were a problem. Like once, I took two hard-rock miners, who worked for Doc Nearhouse at his mine up Palmer Creek, to Seward. They were in Seward about four days spending money like mad men, drinking and chasing women. After the money was all gone and they were both half sick, they were ready to go back to Hope to work. They took a bottle along to sober up with and I started to Hope with them. They had a drink every once in awhile. When I stopped to leave off some groceries at Bert Higgins', who was an old prospector at Mile 44, Carl Lund asked him if he wanted a drink. Bert accepted the offer real quick and Carl handed him the bottle. I guess it was 120 proof rum or something pretty strong. Bert took a couple big gulps of that sutff and then his eyes watered and he started gasping for breath and saying, "G-G-G-Go-God tha-that's go-good." It must have set him on fire.

I got over along Turnagain Arm when Irish had to get out and "mark up the snow" (in other words pee), but "mark up the snow" was an old sourdough saying. I stopped the truck at a spot along the road that was fifteen feet from a thirty-foot drop right into Turnagain Arm. The tide was in with big chunks of ice floating around. When he opened the truck door I realized he was drunk from hitting the bottle too much. He just fell out but tried to get his feet under himself so was stumbling and running right toward Turnagain Arm. I just dived over Carl's lap and grabbed Irish by the feet, and pulled him down in the snow about eight feet from the bluff. He got up madder than a bear wanting to fight and Carl and I finally got him calmed down. It was a pretty big scare. I sure thought he was a goner.

One time when I was making a round trip to Seward a fellow by the name of Bill wanted to go along for a quick trip. I never passed anyone up that was walking along the road, so about a mile out of Moose Pass I stopped and asked a lady if she wanted to ride. She was pretty well painted up, not bad looking, and I could see she was a stranger in the country. I found out she was pretty well intoxicated too. She introduced herself as "The Texas Queen". I found out later she had been shacking up with some of the old boys along the railroad and had stayed all night with a section hand at Moose Pass, and now she wanted to get to Seward. That was just fine; we were going that way. I hadn't gone down the road two miles when she kind of giggled a couple of times and said, "You will think I am awful, but I have to go."

I stopped, figuring she would go out in the brush. No way, Boy! She left the truck door open and just squatted down right there on the road. I looked at Bill, and grinned, and nudged him with my elbow. He rolled his eyes and said, "God, what a character." All the rest of the way to Seward Bill and I were sure elbowing each other over the things we talked about. She was a lot different than most people I picked up. When I stopped at the street corner to let her and Bill out, Bill stayed in the truck. He was not going to be seen getting out of my truck with "The Texas Queen". Ha!

Every once in awhile one of the men in Hope, Moose Pass or along the road would stop me and say, "My wife is having a birthday. Will you get her something?" It never did any good to ask what I should get because they would just say, "Oh! look around. You pick out something." When I got to Seward I would go into Mrs. Blue's ladies apparel store and buy panties, a new slip, nightgown or stockings. Mrs. Blue would ask what size. I would say, "Just a minute", and keep looking out on the street. When I saw a woman go by about the size of the lady I was buying for, I would tell Mrs. Blue, "That lady's size", and it generally always worked out real well. It was always a mystery to those men though how I knew their wifes' sizes. The women all got a big kick out of some of the things I bought for them. It always put the husbands in good standing.

Mr. Swetman sure did have a laugh on me one time. I just was not thinking I guess. He asked what I would charge him to get some old ore car tracks up from Palmer Creek canyon, where we had been placer mining, and haul them up to Hershey's mine. Someone had a high grade prospect of gold ore on the other side of Palmer Creek from where we placer-mined, and it had petered out so the hard-rock mine was abandoned. I told him real quick like it would cost seventy-five dollars. He said, "Do it." There were about sixty pieces of thirty-foot long, fifteen-pound rails that were down this steep three-hundred-foot bank. I had to drag them up on top, then load and haul them ten miles up the creek. I got Louis, my brother-in-law, to help me. It took two days to get them delivered, but Mr. Swetman knew I took that job too cheap.

The gold that was in the hard-rock mine was a pretty green gold, in little long crystals. You could see between the crystals as though they were held together by a magnet. When we were placer mining on Palmer Creek we got some pretty good sized sliver nuggets about the size of date seeds.

I got along pretty well with all the people, but a couple of times I got my dander up. Flora had been in the hospital a lot that summer and I was behind on my debt to the hospital. One day I met a gal, I won't call her a lady, whom I knew by just seeing on the street in Seward sometimes. She came up to me on the street in front of the Seward Hardware and said, "Mr. McCart, I am now in charge of the Red Cross in Seward." I said, "Well, that's nice. I wish you all the luck in the world." She said again, in a loud voice, "I am in charge of the Red Cross."

About that time Gus Johnson came out by the door of the hardware store to listen in. He knew I was having trouble with my bills at the hospital, and thought maybe the Red Cross was a pretty good outfit and would help me with some bills. I was thinking the same thing about them. For about five minutes every time somebody came by she would repeat about me having a hard time and how the Red Cross helped people. I finally got the drift and was I mad. I told her real quick she did not have to stand on the street and try to get advertisement by embarrassing me. I told her to just go over and pay the hospital some money, and I would give her plenty of advertising. She went down the street at a pretty good pace. Gus grinned and said, "Good for you, Dennie. She had it coming." The Red Cross did not pay any of my bills, and I have never done any advertising for them in the right way either.

When I was hauling some hewed railroad ties to the Lawing siding, from Pack Olsen's, I learned some more about the old time sourdoughs. Hank Frost and Pack Olsen were visiting one evening when I was staying there while hauling ties. They were talking about when they were working for the Government Geodetic Survey in the early days. They talked about the time they were out of meat and all the men were getting tired of just beans, sourdough hot cakes and biscuits. One night while camping near a swamp they took turns watching for a moose to come out so they could get meat for camp. After two of the men had put in a two-hour stand each it was Pack's turn to watch. At two thirty AM everybody was awakened by a rifle shot and Pack hollering to the fellows to get up and help him dress the moose; "By God I got one." They were all happy and took off over to where Pack had killed the moose. Lo and behold, Pack had killed one of their pack mules. It got loose somehow from the pack horses and mules and wandered into the swamp. They said the mule didn't taste bad, but it was sure tough. Hank told me the reason they called Olsen "Pack" was because anytime they were moving camp and had some last things to put on a packboard, they always put it on Olsen's. He was a big, powerful man, and packed anything he could stand under.

I laughed when they were talking about one winter when they were on the trail together and stopped at a trapper's cabin for the night. The trapper had some dang good stew, and Pack said it was sure good until Hank started to take a second helping, and a muskrat tailfell on the plate. Oh Boy!

I could have sat up all night listening to these two old guys talk about the old days on the trail.

These three little girls, Martha, Shirley and Arlene, got a big kick out of climbing over the stile at the fence between Mitchells' and my place, and this day they stopped in to visit Flora. Arlene was looking all around the room, scared, so Flora asked her what was wrong. Arlene said, "I am not supposed to be in your house. You have germs, but I don't see any." Bless her little heart. It did strike Flora kind of funny, and she got a big laugh out of it. When I got home that night she had to tell me about the visit.

Alice Mitchell had to pin a sign on the back of Martha's coat saying, "Send me home at 4 P.M.", because Martha would never come home in time for supper. That way, whoever she was visiting would tell her it was time for her to go home. Early in the fall the women of Hope had a party every month. They had written a play to be put on at the Hope Social Hall. This would start the winter season of fun and good times. There were sixteen women in the play. It was a good show of different things that went on during the summer.

We men decided we would have to do something to outdo the women, so Mitchell started talking about a minstrel show. After two weeks of writing, and talking to all the men, we went to the hall and did some practicing. We blacked up like Negroes, and tried to talk like Negroes, but it was pretty funny to hear someone with a Swedish accent talking southern Negro talk. We started the show with the hall full of people, and half of Moose Pass was there.

We had Louis playing the guitar, and Louie Shell singing "The Husky Dusky Maiden Way Up North" with an Eskimo and Negro accent. Boy! it was funny, and it was good as he had a very nice voice. Mitchell and Carl Clark kept talking about the jug Carl had. It was hard cider, and Carl knew it was, because it had eaten up an iron wedge and now it was ready to drink. He had something pretty hard in it all right. He passed it around and everybody had a drink, and it was pretty warm stuff. The second time around we could feel it.

Mr. Brenner told some funny jokes. I played the violin left-handed, and did some yodeling. I found some high notes I never knew I had after getting my throat cleared out with that hard cider. George Roll got up to give a political speech trying to speak Negro with a German accent. That was terrific, and he was real serious at this political speech which made it more fun.

When the show was over and everybody applauded, they were surprised to see only two Negro men left up front when we opened the curtains. The Moose Pass boys were looking forward to getting a swig of Carl's hard cider. We all climbed out the window behind the curtain and went home to wash the black from our faces. We had a dance after the show and I am sure the Moose Pass people had a good time. The Moose Pass boys got some of Carl's hard cider, too.

Before the show I went up to Sunrise to get Mike Connely. He was the only old sourdough in Sunrise at that time. We called him the Mayor of Sunrise. In the gold rush days around 1908 there was a tent town of five thousand people living there.

He was a very good dancer, and a dignified Irish gentleman. Everybody liked him. It really floored Flora and I when Mike got out of the truck and thanked us for a good time. Then with a twinkle in his eye he said, "You kids go straight home now." Flora and I laughed all the way home.

One time after that Mike was at our potluck dinner and dance. After eating we had some entertainment, and we asked anyone who was new to join in if they wished. This night in particular we had a Forest Service gentleman who volunteered to sing. Bob Davis accompanied him on the guitar. He was a wonderful singer, and we sure enjoyed a couple of songs by him. Then Mike Connely came up and asked Bob to sound a certain key on the guitar; then he started singing in an Irish tenor the song, "Sweet Forget-Me-Not". Boy! Oh Boy! this old sourdough had sung on the stage, or to many a moose in his early days. It was beautiful. He would sing loud, and then low and sweet; just made tears come to your eyes. No one will ever forget that singing by an old man like that.

We had some grand times at this old hall. There were three bunk beds in the corner of the hall where the small children slept while we all danced until we decided to go home. Sometimes it would be 3 o'clock in the morning. We were very happy to have people like Swede Gresham, Harry Johnson and Peter Hatch come and play with us. I had the privilege of playing with them all. Bea Davis would also come out from Seward and join us with her violin and saxophone. "Sentimental Journey" was her favorite tune. Hub Clark picked a five-string banjo. I sure liked to play the violin with him.

It was a very big shock to me when Carl came to my door at 4 o'clock in the morning and told me Pap was dead. He died of heart failure real sudden, and Carl wanted me to pick up a coffin in Seward for him. He was buried on the hill on Carl's property. All the people of Hope were there to bid Hub goodbye and happy hunting on the trail beyond. It was a funeral that had a feeling so dear to everybody there.

One day when I was up Resurrection Creek road I stopped by Shobe's homestead as I was going to take some packages up to the mines. Dorothy came out and told me she had taken a job cooking at Carl's mine and was scared she would be a failure. She had never cooked for a crew of men before and didn't know very much about baking bread, etc. She wanted to know what did I think about it. I said, "Don't worry, there is only one thing to remember. Just cook lots of food as those guys will be plenty hungry and eat anything." She turned out to be a dang good cook. All the men spoke well of the food. It was a good job for her as they needed the money. Homesteading was not too profitable a business in those days. She was wondering if she should endorse her check for almost five hundred dollars for the season's work and turn it over to me to get cashed in Seward, but I guess some of the people convinced her she could trust me. I did get to cash the check and give her the hard-earned money.

It was four days before Thanksgiving and I had to make a quick trip to Seward to get turkeys for people along the road and at Hope. My truck had a universal joint go out so I borrowed Turpin's truck and Turpin went to Seward with me. We got the turkeys from the meat market and started home.

It was a mild day and the road was slick when we left Moose Pass about 5 PM. We passed two cars coming to Moose Pass, and in less than four minutes after we passed those cars we came around the corner by Weaver's little house. There was the biggest snowslide I had ever seen. It was fifteen to twenty feet thick and about one hundred feet across. The snow was just settling down. Boy! it's just a miracle we were not under that snow. We turned around and went back to Moose Pass and told Roy Thurston, the road foreman, about the snowslide. He said they would make preparations to get it out the next morning and we could stay with them for the night. Mrs. Thurston had two more men to cook for. We could not pay her for our lodging the next morning when we left. We went out to the slide and found out it would be two or three days before we could drive to Hope. We packed the turkeys and packages across the slide where Bill Saxton was waiting. He lived at Mile 50 so he took us to Hope. Everybody had their turkey for Thanksgiving and we were thankful to be alive.

That winter Turpin with his truck and trailer, and I with my truck and trailor, were busy hauling piling that he was cutting for the army. We tried to pick the weather and would make two trips a day to Moose Pass when possible. Gee! at night up on the summit all the bushes were shining with big diamonds of sparkling frost. Sometimes, for fun, I would pick out a couple special big ones for Flora and I.

One night I got to Moose Pass about three o'clock in the morning. It was around zero and a bright clear night. The Northern Lights were putting on a show above the mountains by Trail Lake. You could see the snow-covered mountains like big mounds of ice cream, two thousand feet high. In the background was a deep blue sky full of big stars, and this magnificent curtain of all the rainbow colors, about

The Snowslide at Weavers.

Dennie McCart Hauling Piling.

A Winter Scene at Mile 50.

two miles wide and one-half mile high, waving back and forth just above the mountain like a breeze blowing a curtain. And there were streaks of orange light shooting up. God was putting on a big stage show. Anyhow you felt like you were seeing something in heaven, and felt real close to God and His handiwork. It was so still that night that you could hear the Northern Lights making a swishing sound. I'll never forget that beautiful sight.

15
We Got Into a Blizzard

One afternoon when I loaded up with piling, the weather looked bad across Turnagain Arm but okay on our side. Turpin's truck was broke down so he thought he would ride with me. We took off for Moose Pass but got into stormy weather just before we got to the summit. We just poured it on, hoping we would get to Moose Pass before the snow got too deep. The weather got worse and the wind started howling along Summit Lake, and by the time we got to Jerome Lake we were in a blizzard. I told Turpin that if we could just across the flats by Tern Lake it would be all downhill, and by the mountains along Trail Lake to Moose Pass we would be able to see better and probably make it. When we got on the flats, with one foot of snow and pulling a trailer, we spun out. We would get out and shovel the snow out by our wheels and ahead away, take a run at it, then wind up doing the same thing again. We were making headway and started to go downhill, but I could hardly see a thing even with the headlights. I could see something, though, that was not the road, and stopped right up against a snowslide. There was no turning around, and we were in dangerous snowslide country. I told Turpin we would have to get out of the truck and go for shelter. We were both dressed warm, with muskrat fur caps on. It was about twenty degrees. If we walked four miles facing the storm we would be in Moose Pass, and if we walked four miles with the storm at our back we would be at Bill Fairman's cabin, which was located at the upper end of Jerome Lake. We decided to go with the wind, and I wrote a note saying it was eleven o'clock at night and we were going to go back to Bill Fairman's cabin, and signed it Turpin and Dennie. I then put the note on the truck key.

We started back along the road and we could tell when we were along the sides of the road, by the snow banks. We were pretty scared as we heard a loud noise every once in awhile, louder than the usual wind and snow. We knew it was snowslides, and just didn't talk about it. At one thirty in the morning two fellows with snow froze to their clothes, and snow and icicles all over their soggy fur caps, staggered up and knocked on the door of Bill Fairman's cabin. He hollered, "Just a minute", and came to the door with a bug in his hand. A bug is a lantern made from a half-gallon lard can with the sides rolled back so as to make a door in front and a wire handle on top, with the tin bottom cut in a cross with the tin bent up so as to hold a candle. It makes a good light and won't blow out in a wind. When he opened the door he was in his long flannel nightgown, and had a night cap on. Gee! he looked good even though it was a funny sight.

He said, "My God, come in out of this blizzard. I have been worried all night about Dennie. He went by here about eight thirty in this storm with a load of piling."

I said, "Bill, who do you think this is?" He held the bug up close to me and Turpin, and then he went into a tizzy. He had us get all our wet clothes off and put on some of his, which were plenty big as he was a tall man. We hung our wet clothes around the stove to dry, and he got some hot soup for us. He waited on us like an old hen with chicks, but we were ready to be waited on about then, so did not put up an argument. We stayed with him two days, resting and waiting for the road men to open the road. Bill would give us our dinner first. He said he had been a bachelor for so long he had developed a habit of sitting by the table sidesaddle, with his legs crossed, and would eat from the table that way. We accepted his method and waited on him in return.

The second day about noon we heard the rotary snowplow and other equipment coming. The road men were happy to see we were okay and well. Roy said my truck and trailer were okay, and that he would take us down to the truck so we could go on to Moose Pass. That night we got

back to Hope and I tell you there were two very happy
wives to know we were okay. Bill would not accept any pay
for our stay with him those two days. He said he enjoyed the
visit and to come back under different conditions, and to
just pass the favor along to someone else sometime.

It was a frustrating time, getting to Seward at night with
everything blacked out, the army on alert, and me trying to
see good enough to get to the hotel to sleep. Then one morning I came into Seward about 9 AM to see half the town
burned to the ground. There was ice, soot, water and people red-eyed and dirty from fire fighting. They were packing peoples' belongings a block away from the fire. What a
pitiful thing to see. I guess it was a good thing I had three
thousand telephone poles to haul. I didn't have time to get
too depressed. Flora was in the hospital again, and it
seemed like with the war, everything was going haywire.

16
Schoolteacher's Problems

That fall we got a new schoolteacher at Hope. It was Mr. Frampton, along with his wife, Margaret, two daughters, Janice and Patsy, and a baby boy, Clayton. They were looking for a way to get to Hope, and the man at the Van Gilder Hotel told them about an orange truck with Hope Truck Line printed on the door. He said that was their man and to just watch for the truck. Dennie was generally in town every day. I was busy hauling to some mines just then, and was not around. They were looking for me two days when they ran across Mr. Nutter, who hauled mail, passengers and freight to Hope. They made arrangements with him to get their freight at the dock and take them to Hope. They never did catch up with the Hope Truck Line until about two weeks later.

Mr. Frampton had taught school for quite a few years in the King Salmon and Dillingham country, so had no trouble getting acquainted and getting school started in Hope. Everybody in town had a good laugh sometime later. Patsy was about Martha Mitchell's age, and they played together a lot. Clayton always tagged along wherever Patsy went. Alice Mitchell had warned Martha to never play around the rainbarrel which was a fifty-gallon gas barrel with one end out, sitting under the rainspout by the house. Alice used this water to water the flowers that were outside. These two little girls were up on a box splashing in the rainbarrel when Alice saw them out the kitchen window. Boy! Oh Boy! she hurried out there scolding and just grabbed Martha by the feet and dunked her in the rainbarrel. Martha came up out of there blubbering and bawling and Alice turned to ask Patsy if she was next. But it was too late. Patsy had grabbed Clayton by the hand and was out to the road already headed for the schoolhouse. Alice Mitchell never had any more kids wanting to play in the rainbarrel after that.

It seemed like every time I came into Hope on my Saturday trip I would wind up at Mitchell's for a sandwich and tea. Mr. Mitchell wanted to catch up on the news along the road so he would ask Alice to make me a sandwich. One time he asked her to make a sandwich and she looked at me kind of funny, then said, "Do you like bread crusts?" I said, "Yep! I sure do." Alice said, "Good, because that's all I have to make a sandwich with." So I got the last two crusts of bread in their house. We have had a big laugh about me and my crusty sandwich ever since.

There was also a cat that adopted me, somehow, in Hope. I talked pussycat talk to her too much. Anyhow, she kept me company when I was home. As soon as I left she would jump over the fence to Mitchell's house and be Martha's cat. We called her Mrs. Murphy. Any time I came into Hope and stopped at the post office, that cat and all the kids would come running. I generally had some funny books from the drugstore, and some candy for the kids. They would ride all around town helping me unload. They were good little swampers. This cat would come running with her tail straight up in the air, jump up on the back of the truck seat, purr, purr, purr, and rub up against my neck. She sure liked to ride in the truck with all of us, and she would be my cat and stay at my house until I left again.

Moose Pass did not have enough children that fall to have a school so some of the kids took correspondence courses; others went to Seward. But around November more kids moved into Moose Pass, and they wanted to open a school. Juneau finally got a schoolteacher from a city somewhere outside, in the U.S., to take the job. She came in on the train and got off at Moose Pass section house. The section foreman pointed down the street about a block where the school was, and told her Mrs. Reed, or the storekeeper across the street had the schoolhouse key. I guess she managed somehow to carry her two heavy suitcases down to Mrs. Reed's and tell her who she was. Mrs. Reed asked her to stay there overnight, and she could go over to the schoolhouse and look things over. Going over to a big, empty, cold schoolhouse with a pump to prime for water was more than she could handle. When she got back to Mrs Reed's house, Mrs. Reed said, "I don't know why someone here had not heard you were coming so we could have the schoolhouse warm and cleaned up for you." She told her that Dennie, the truck driver who always hauled stove oil and coal for the school, would be there the next morning about 10 o'clock and she would send me right over.

When I got to the Moose Pass store, Mrs. Reed came over to tell me the new schoolteacher wanted to see me. When I got to the schoolhouse, I saw that nice looking schoolteacher standing in the cold room, scared to death. I started to ask a few questions about why some of the people had not come over to show her how to start the oil stove and get the pump working. She started to cry and told me about living in a city, and how she didn't know anything about taking care of a schoolhouse. She just knew how to teach. I told her I was sorry about the way Moose Pass had welcomed her, and told her the best thing she could do was to get on the train in about an hour, and go to Anchorage, and get a job there as a teacher or secretary. There were plenty of jobs there. She could phone or write Juneau and explain what she was up against in Moose Pass. That's all it took. Like a flash she had me go over to Reed's, leave the key, get her suitcases and take her to the section house, and when the train came, she went to Anchorage. I don't know how she made out there, but I hope everything worked out for her.

Within a week Juneau sent another teacher by the name of Orah Dee Clark. She was a teacher from the early days who had taught in the interior and all over the territory. She came down from Anchorage, and when she got off the train, she was gathering kindling wood so when she got to the schoolhouse she could start a fire in the cook stove. She got Floyd Wolfe over to prime the pump and get the oil stoves going. The next morning she rang the schoolbell and school was on its way. When I came through there a few days later I got acquainted with her. She was a real sour-dough schoolmarm, and any person who knew her knew a wonderful lady and a darn good teacher.

17
Snow River Country

About once a year there was a very unusual thing that would happen at Snow River. Sometimes it would flood in the fall, early spring, or middle of winter, even when there was no storm or anything to cause a flood. When the flood came it filled the whole valley one-fourth mile with water. At Mile 18 where the road crossed the valley they had a bridge, and then piling with trestle about half the distance across the valley, to let all this water through into Kenai Lake.

Kenai Lake was thirty miles long and around a mile wide. To give you an idea of how much water came down Snow River at this flood time, the lake would rise four or five feet. That is millions of acre feet of water.

The engineers and survey people went up Snow River Valley, to the head, to see where all this water came from. What happens is that there is a big glacier about twenty miles long and eight miles wide with mountain tops on each side. Down under this glacier, where the river runs out, is a big opening. And under this glacier is a big empty valley, or lake, that fills up when the ice falls down, and plugs the river where it runs out from underneath the glacier. After six months or a year, you never know when, the plug gives way and there is another flood.

The winter of 1943 we had a whopper of a flood. It washed the bridge out, and no traffic got across for three weeks until piling was driven and a temporary bridge built. I left my truck on the Seward side and packed the packages and necessary freight across on the ice after the water went down to normal. I was able to borrow Kent King's new Ford pickup to run my route on the Hope side. The other five days of each week I got a job with the road crew to help

build the bridge. Mr. and Mrs. Fred Laubscher asked me to
stay with them, and they asked Flora to come and stay, too.
Flora was in the hospital at that time, and Mrs. Laubscher
wanted to take care of her and help me with my expenses, so
I brought her out to their home. It was such a pretty place
by Trail Lake, and we really enjoyed the stay with them. It
was like a vacation, and was appreciated very, very much.

One day I got word that Mr. George Roll had died in his
sleep. Mrs. Roll wanted me to get an undertaker and a coffin, and come to Hope to get Mr. Roll as he wanted to be
buried in Seward. I got the undertaker and coffin at Seward
and came out to where we walked across the ice, and then
took King's pickup to Hope. The weather was turning
warm, and we encountered slick icy roads, but got to Hope
and picked up Mr. Roll then started back for Seward. By
that time the roads were plenty slick. We had a very scary
ride. The undertaker said he rode about halfway with his
eyes shut, and prayed for me and the dead man. We packed
the coffin across the ice at Snow River, and there was some
water running over the ice at that time. I got the trip com-
pleted about 7 PM. I got a bite to eat and went back to
Fred's house, getting there around 9 PM, plenty tired and
ready to get some rest.

The next morning I was to go to work with Fred on the
bridge. We had all crossed on the ice that morning and
started to work. Roy asked me to go across and get a peavey
as I had hip boots on and could wade the water that was
running over the ice about fourteen inches deep. I got on the
other side and got the peavey, then started back. Boy! Oh!
Boy! about ten feet from shore I stepped off into the cold icy
water, over my head. I spun around and came up on the ice
faster than a seal could have done. The men looked surprised. Then all at once a big chunk of ice twenty feet wide
and forty feet long came floating past where we were going
to drive piling. Oh! Man! was I cold. I had some clothes in
the truck that I had picked up at the laundry in Seward so I
went to the truck and changed clothes, and then went back
to work. We had to use a boat to cross until the bridge was

finished. I told the men we were sure lucky the night before when the undertaker and I were crossing the ice. It would have been a calamity if we would have fallen through the ice while packing the coffin with George Roll in it. I am sure we did not need to be baptized at that time of the year. The reason the stay at Fred Laubscher's meant so much to me was that it was the last happy vacation Flora and I had together. Early that fall Doctor Banister had a specialist stop in Seward and see what could be done for Flora. After a thorough examination, and an effort to inflate her one lung, Doctor Banister told me, "Dennie, you might just as well realize that Flora is not going to be with you much longer." After a few minutes I was able to tell Doctor Banister that the last few months I was afraid for her and I felt so helpless. Then I went on my way hoping and praying a miracle could happen. I worked long hours and I seemed to just about live in the truck. I would be driving along the beautiful country around Summit Lake when I would stare off into the blue sky above the pretty mountains and ask God to please help us, but I guess He wanted Flora more than I. You can see why this stay at Fred Laubscher's meant so much to me, and they never took a penny for our stay there.

I had a terrible experience with a new health nurse who had just arrived in Seward. She was checking up on people in town, and she had talked to Flora while making her visit to the hospital. She had left word with Bob Trotter, who was the storekeeper at McMullen's store, that she wanted to see me. When I came into the store Bob told me about her. I perked up and said, "Gee! Bob, maybe she can help Flora and me." I had been trying to get Flora into a sanatorium in the "South 48". All the places wanted me to guarantee four hundred dollars a month in advance, and I just couldn't afford it.

I went right over to the post office and up the steps to her office on the second floor. Her office was at the end of the hall. The Forest Service and Judge Bryant's offices were first, and they all had their doors open. I said "howdy" to the Forest Service men, and to Judge Bryant, then walked into the office where a nice looking lady sat at her desk. I introduced myself and told her I got her message that she wanted to see me. She got up and put her hands on her hips and started out in a loud voice. "Mr. McCart, you should be ashamed of yourself letting that beautiful young girl lay over in that hospital day after day by herself while you are out enjoying life." Oh Boy! by then I had my Irish really steamed up and was kind of shocked, but madder than hell. So I said in a loud voice, that could be heard all over the building, "Just a Goddamn minute you bitch you! What the hell is the matter with you? You don't know what you are talking about! Don't you ever tell me I am not helping or doing all that I can possibly do for Flora, and if I ever hear another word that you say about us I will kick the hell right out of you!" I turned around and started down the hall. Never did I ever talk to anybody like that before, or ever since. But she had it coming. There stood Judge Bryant. He said, "Good for you, Dennie". The two Forest Service men were staring out the door wondering what had happened. I guess the smoke followed me for hours before I cooled off. Anyhow, I only saw that gal once downtown, and she cut across the street to avoid me. I never knew just what happened in Seward, but they must have requested she move on.

Early that spring the Mathison brothers were finishing the construction of a nice big power barge, and had ordered two new Chevrolet-six engines for the power source. It was a difficult job to purchase things like that with the war and all, but with Pete Ogle, the Emergency Board and myself we were able to get the motors for them. I was very happy to deliver the two new motors to them.

18
Flora's Death

On April 23, 1944, I got into Seward, placed all my orders, then went to the hospital to see Flora. Hannah Lupin was the nurse on duty and she told me Flora was very sick and had been asking for me. When I went in the room I was in a cold sweat and took her hand telling her it was Dennie. I am not sure if she knew or not as she was breathing little breaths, saying in a low voice, "Oh! Oh!" She must have been suffering something terrible. Hannah came in about then and felt of Flora's feet and pulse, then looked at me with very sad eyes. She told me I had better take a walk for a few minutes. She could see tears in my eyes. I saw Flora alive for the last time, through tears. I walked out into the hall and up the stairs to the waiting room. I just sat down in a chair when Rev. Knight came in and asked me how Flora was. All I remember doing is just giving him a shoulder shrug and looking up. He must have known as he just zoomed down the steps. There I sat helpless as could be and in about five minutes I heard footsteps coming up the stairs. It was Hannah. She came to me with a very sorry look and said, "Dennie, Flora is not suffering anymore. She is gone."

I remember telling Hannah that Dr. Banister had told me to prepare for this, but no way can a person do it till he has to.

I went out to the truck and sat there holding the steering wheel and rubbing the dash, as if it was the only thing I had left, with 125,000 miles on the speedometer all traveled on just about ninety miles of road. After sitting there about ten minutes I drove over to where Flora's folks lived and told Mrs. Shell and the children that Flora was gone. Mrs. Shell went out into the kitchen to cry, and the children followed as they were concerned over their mother crying, so there I sat all alone again. Finally I got a hold of myself and told them goodbye. I drove over to the Seward Hotel, got a room and went upstairs to start thinking of what I would do about the funeral arrangements; and to go right on with my trucking business as usual. This is when I thought back to my younger days when my dad had told me, "Kid, remember: working, laughing and sorrow, you must go on till death." I have used those words many times.

Mrs. Oscar Dahl knocked on my door about thirty minutes after I went upstairs telling me I had a phone call. I went down and it was Mrs. Stafford calling from Moose Pass asking me to pick up some freight from McMullin's store the next morning. Then she asked how Flora was. Oh Boy! those tears started flowing but I managed to say, "I am sorry to say, but she just died about one hour ago." Mrs. Stafford was silent for a few seconds then said in a sad voice, "Dennie, I am so sorry", and hung up. Mrs. Dahl stood there in shock and we did not have to say anything. I just went back up to my room to try to get some rest and be ready for tomorrow. The next morning after breakfast I went into the McMullin's store to talk to them about funeral arrangements as they owned the funeral parlor. Bob Trotter said he had heard about Flora's death, and everybody in Seward was sorry. After a few minutes with Bob Trotter all arrangements were made and I got busy with my business as usual, repeating the words, "Onward through life we must go." There were not many words said about Flora being gone, all I had to do was just see those people and know how they felt.

The Mukluk Telegraph had worked again; all seventy-five miles of my big family heard the sad news. In three days Flora's funeral was held at the Lutheran Church in Seward. The church was filled with all our friends, and Rev. Knight gave the euology and Mrs. Blue sang two songs. I saw Flora for the last time resting in peace.

19
Selling The Hope Truck Line

Within a few weeks I decided to sell my truck line and try something else. I needed a few thousand dollars to pay up my bills so I ran an ad in the paper and also told the businessmen around Seward that I was selling. In no time at all I had three interested men. I finally came to an agreement with Bill Brattain. I took him on the route introducing him to the people and showing him the business. I will always remember the remark Mr. Swetman made to Bill Brattain when I told him about the sale. He said, "I don't know a thing about you Mr. Brattain. But just remember, there is no way you can take Dennie's place on this truck line."

In a few weeks I paid the Seward Hospital twelve hundred dollars which I owed. The gentleman who was bookkeeper at the hospital was once the head of the U.S.O. in Seward. He said to me, "Dennie, if everybody paid their bills at this hospital like you, we would sure be happy. I am giving back to you twenty dollars to show our appreciation." I have wondered ever since. I bet he paid that out of his own pocket. Anyhow, I sure thought it was pretty nice. It was all the money I had in my purse and maybe he noticed that. And anyway, I had a big feed with some of that twenty dollars. Thank you, Sir, wherever you are.

Bob Mathison wrote a poem about me selling my truck line which I want to share with you.